ADVANCES IN PSYCHOANALYSIS

Advances
in Psychoanalysis

CONTRIBUTIONS TO

KAREN HORNEY'S HOLISTIC APPROACH

Edited and with an Introduction

by HAROLD KELMAN, M.D.

New York

W · W · NORTON & COMPANY · INC ·

COPYRIGHT © 1964 BY W. W. NORTON & COMPANY, INC.

FIRST EDITION

Library of Congress Catalog Card No. 64-11133

Published simultaneously in the Dominion of
Canada by George J. McLeod Limited, Toronto

PRINTED IN THE UNITED STATES OF AMERICA
FOR THE PUBLISHERS BY THE VAIL-BALLOU PRESS, INC.

1 2 3 4 5 6 7 8 9

DISCARD

CONTENTS

INTRODUCTION

In his Presidential Statement before the International Psychoanalytic Association in May 1936, while Freud was still alive, Ernest Jones, one of his first and most loyal colleagues, said, "In the field of Theory . . . I am inclined to anticipate very considerable changes in the course of the next twenty years or so. The scaffolding, as he modestly called it, that Freud has erected, has stood much rough weather extraordinarily well, though he has had to repair and strengthen it from time to time. But it would be counter to all our knowledge of the history and essential nature of science to suppose that it will not be extensively modified with the passage of time. The preconceptions from the world of contemporary scientific thought . . . with which Freud approached his studies had a visible influence on his theoretical structure, and they necessarily bear the mark of a given period. We must expect that other workers, schooled by different disciplines than his, will be able to effect fresh orientations, to formulate fresh correlations. In spite of our natural piety we must brace ourselves to welcome such changes, fortifying ourselves with the reflection that to face new truth and to hold truth above all other consideration had been Freud's greatest lesson to us

and his most precious legacy to psychological science." [1]
Karen Horney is a unique example of Jones's prophecy.
She received her medical degree in 1913 from the University of Berlin. During World War I, she continued with
her psychiatric and psychoanalytic studies in Berlin. A
new period in the psychoanalytic movement opened when
the Berlin Psychoanalytic Institute was founded in 1920;
Horney taught there until 1932. With her were many of
those who were to create what would be the history of
psychoanalysis in Europe and the United States. In 1932
Franz Alexander asked her to become the Associate Director of the Chicago Psychoanalytic Institute. In 1934
she came to New York as a member of the teaching staff of
the Psychoanalytic Institute. All through her life—in Berlin, Chicago and New York—Horney was at the vital center
of the psychoanalytic movement.

In New York, Horney's ideas and the ideas of others, as
well as their wish for greater freedom of discussion and
investigation, were met by orthodoxy's increasing restrictiveness. In 1941, a number of members and candidates-in-training of the Institute, as well as members of the American Psychoanalytic Association in other cities, withdrew to
form the Association for the Advancement of Psychoanalysis under Horney's leadership. In it she played a crucial
role as the founding Dean of the American Institute for
Psychoanalysis where she taught and was a training analyst,
and as the founding Editor of *The American Journal of
Psychoanalysis* in which many of her contributions appeared.

Shortly after her death in 1952, C. P. Oberndorf wrote
in the *International Journal of Psycho-analysis* that there

[1] Rado, S., Grinker, Sr., R.R., and Alexander, F.: Editorial, *Arch.
Gen. Psychiat.* 8, 1963.

had "passed from the psychoanalytic scene a distinguished, vigorous and independent figure. . . . There seems little doubt that Horney retained a strong devotion to Freud's procedure of a thoroughgoing investigation of psychic conflict and did not sacrifice conscientious work with patients to rapid or superficial methods."

In 1917 in Berlin Horney wrote her first paper, "The Technique of Psychoanalytic Therapy." [2] "The analytical theories," she stated, "have grown out of observations and experiences which were made in applying this method. The theories, in turn, later exerted their influence on the practice." From this pure research viewpoint she never deviated; theories must be considered as provisional conveniences, always to be tested against facts. She concluded this paper with, "Psychoanalysis can free a human being who was tied hands and feet. It cannot give him new arms or legs. Psychoanalysis, however, has shown us that much that we have regarded as constitutional merely represents a blockage of growth, a blockage which can be lifted." Thus Horney's philosophy was already evident—growth centered and life affirmative. Her holistic concept of blockage of growth contrasted with Freud's mechanistic notion of resistance. She was already ranging herself against the organic orientation toward mental illness which saw constitution as immutable; she saw it rather as a dynamic possibility, a concept later expanded by Ernst Kretschmer against the background of his classic *Körperbau und Charakter (Body Structure and Character)*.[3] Horney also saw

[2] *"Die Technik der psychoanalytischen Therapie." Zeitschr. f. Sexualwissenschaft,* IV, 1917.

[3] Kretschmer, E. *The Image of Man in Psychotherapy. The American Journal of Psychoanalysis* (Karen Horney Memorial Issue) XIV, 1, 1954.

that much that had been considered constitutional was the outcome of distorting growth possibilities and the energies available for them into sick defensive attitudes, which in turn blocked those possibilities. The contrast between Horney's holistic orientation and Freud's pessimistic, materialistic, constitutional and sex-centered philosophy was clearly evident in 1917.

She also found herself in opposition to other basic tenets of Freudian psychology. In the first of a series of papers on so-called feminine psychology (1922), she took issue with the basic premise of Abraham's ideas on penis envy and castration complex in women.[4] In "The Flight from Womanhood"[5] (1926) she added, "The new point of view came to me by way of philosophy in some essays of Georg Simmel" who asserted that the very standards by which mankind had estimated the values of male and female nature are "not neutral, arising out of difference of sexes, but in themselves essentially masculine. . . . I, as a woman, ask in amazement: And what about motherhood? And the blissful consciousness of bearing a new life within oneself? And the ineffable happiness of the increasing expectation of the appearance of this new being? And the joy when it finally makes its appearance and one holds it for the first time in one's arms? And the deep pleasurable feeling of satisfaction in suckling it and the happiness of the whole period when the infant needs her care?" In asking these questions, and in her later formulations, Horney opened

[4] *"Zur Genese des Weiblichen Kastrationcomplexes." Internat. Zeitschr. f. Psychoanal.* IX, 1923 ("On the Genesis of the Castration Complex in Women." *Int. J. Psychoanal.* V, Part 1, 1924).

[5] *"Flucht aus der Weiblichkeit." Internat. Zeitschr. f. Psychoanal.* XII, 1926 ("The Flight from Womanhood." *Int. J. Psychoanal.* VII, 1926).

up an entirely new field in the investigation of female psychology. This sequence of papers was a reaction and a necessity. Freud's "anatomy is destiny" had to be confronted, a so-called feminine psychology conceived and transcended, to prepare the way for a whole-person philosophy.

In 1932 when she came to America, the most important and productive phase of Horney's career began. In *New Ways in Psychoanalysis* (1939) she says, "The greater freedom from dogmatic beliefs which I found in this country alleviated the obligation of taking psychoanalytical theories for granted, and gave me the courage to proceed along the lines which I considered right. Furthermore, acquaintance with a culture which in many ways is different from the European taught me to realize that many neurotic conflicts are ultimately determined by cultural conditions." With her new freedom, and with growing assurance of the validity of her own views, Horney also said in *The Neurotic Personality of Our Time* (1937)—"I believe that deference for Freud's gigantic achievements should show itself in building on the foundations that he has laid, and that in this way we can help to fulfill the possibilities which psychoanalysis has for the future, as a theory as well as a therapy. . . . It is possible for the specialist and even for the layman to test the validity of my statements. If he is an attentive observer he can compare my assumptions with his own observations and experience, and on this basis reject or accept, modify or underscore what I have said."

Horney knew and had worked for many years with Freud's theories as he evolved them. She now brought out into the open some of their inadequacies. She had earned the right to stand on the shoulders of her elders and from there could see beyond.

Horney considered infantile anxiety neither the sole sufficient nor necessary cause of later neurotic development because cultural factors might enhance or mitigate it. In the childhood history of adult neurotics she found that there had been a lack of genuine warmth, arousing hostility in the child which had had to be repressed, thereby reinforcing existing anxiety. The resultant feeling "is an insidiously increasing, all-pervading feeling of being lonely and helpless in a hostile world. The acute individual reactions to individual provocations crystallize into a character attitude. This attitude as such does not constitute neurosis but it is the nutritive soil out of which a definite neurosis may develop at any time. Because of the fundamental role this attitude plays in neuroses I have given it a special designation: the basic anxiety; it is inseparably interwoven with a basic hostility." The concept of basic anxiety is further elaborated in *The Neurotic Personality of Our Time*. It reflects existential thinking two decades before it found expression in the United States, and is a first statement of her unique contribution to the understanding of alienation.

New Ways in Psychoanalysis (1939) was the outcome of Horney's awareness that the time had come for her to set down in detail her position with reference to Freud. The book's opening statement is, "My desire to make a critical re-evaluation of psychoanalytic theories had its origin in a dissatisfaction with therapeutic results." She later adds, "The more I took a critical stand toward a series of psychoanalytical theories, the more I realized the constructive value of Freud's fundamental findings and the more paths opened up for the understanding of psychological problems."

On which of Freud's "fundamental findings" did Horney

build, and with which did she differ? Only when "we cut loose from certain historically determined premises" can psychoanalysis "outgrow the limitations set by its being an instinctivistic and a genetic psychology." Horney radically differed with Freud on his notion of the death instinct; but even some of his most loyal disciples would not go along with him from his first promulgation of it. Further, Horney did not see "ego" as a neurotic phenomenon as did Freud, but as a universal one. Years later Freudians credited Horney with having stimulated their developments in ego psychology, which, Ruth Munroe said, "Horney has been shouting from the housetops for twenty years." Sex does not determine character but the character structure determines sexual attitudes and behavior. Horney exposed Freud's methodological error of *pars pro toto* and did not commit the other error of *toto pro pars*.

The differences between Freud's and Horney's attitudes toward moral questions illuminated how wide the gap had become. Dictated by nineteenth century scientific premises Freud could only insist that moral values had no place in a science of psychoanalysis. Horney, intuitively guided by the open-ended thinking of twentieth century science, moved moral issues into a central position. Human destructiveness of self and others is a manifestation of sickness, not of a death or id instinct; guilt feelings are not the outcome of a harsh super-ego but an emotional problem to be understood in the light of healthy moral judgment; and the goal of therapy becomes a moral one, "to restore the individual to himself, to help him regain his spontaneity and find his center of gravity in himself."

Horney found "as the most fundamental and most significant of Freud's findings his doctrines that psychic processes are strictly determined, that actions and feelings may be determined by unconscious motivations and that the motivations driving us are emotional forces." She also found significant Freud's concept of repression, his elucidation of the meaningfulness of dreams, his pointing out that neuroses are the result of conflicts, that anxiety plays a central role in neurosis and that childhood experiences have a crucial significance for neurotic development. The concepts of resistance and transference, and the technique of free association she regarded as among Freud's most valuable contributions. But in *New Ways in Psychoanalysis* and in her later writings her formulation of these issues varied from those of Freud.

Horney was now in a position to develop ideas which were more and more at variance with orthodoxy. Always responsive to the data of clinical practice by which previous hypotheses were tested, she saw the necessity for constant reformulation. These were the areas of her interest and her métier. But she was to play more than the role of a theoretician; the response to her two books and the current trends within and outside the psychoanalytic movement propelled her into the leadership of the Association for the Advancement of Psychoanalysis.

Self-Analysis (1942) was written during that difficult period before and during the founding of the Association. Having dealt with polemics in *New Ways in Psychoanalysis* she now moved into a phase of search and clarification. Around the theme of self-analysis that had concerned many other pioneers, including Freud, she further developed her ideas about neurotic trends. She saw them as attempted solutions to earlier difficulties which, in turn, created additional problems. They determined a person's self-image, namely, that which he would both value and despise. Being incompatible, the trends created further anxieties and conflicts. "My contention is that the conflict born of incompatible attitudes constitutes the core of neurosis and therefore deserves to be called *basic*."

To cope with basic anxiety, the outcome of early disturbed relations, the child develops neurotic character attitudes. "When moving *toward* people he accepts his helplessness. . . . When he moves *against* people he accepts and takes for granted the hostility around him, and determines, consciously or unconsciously, to fight. . . . When he moves *away from* people he wants neither to belong nor to fight, but keeps apart." Horney classified these three moves as compliant, aggressive, and detached, but warned that all types are mixed and that the basis for establishing a typology is too narrow.

The neurotic's attempts at the solution of basic conflicts create an increasingly unstable equilibrium requiring "auxiliary approaches to artificial harmony." These attempts must, of course, fail and the consequences are a host of fears; impoverishment of the personality through a waste of energies; indecisiveness, ineffectualness and inertia; and an impairment of moral integrity with diminished sincerity and increased egocentricity, denied by a variety of unconscious pretenses, and leading to unconscious arrogance. "Hopelessness is an ultimate product of unresolved conflicts," Horney adds, with "the despair of ever being wholehearted and undivided." The aims of therapy must therefore be the resolution of these neurotic conflicts "by changing those conditions within the personality that brought them into being." The goals of therapy are "ideals to strive for . . . *responsibility* . . . *inner independence* . . . *spontaneity of feeling* . . . *wholeheartedness*."

With *Our Inner Conflicts* (1945) moral issues assume increasing importance in Horney's work. Neurosis is moral deterioration brought into being and fostered by moral impairment in human relations. Hopelessness, sadism, egocentricity and arrogance are defined in moral terms. The goals and aim of therapy are clearly questions of ultimate morality, to be distinguished from destructive moralizing and being righteously moralistic.

"A Morality of Evolution" opens *Neurosis and Human Growth* (1950), the culmination of all her previous work. Man's essential nature and spontaneous morality are inextricably one, thereby defining sickness, health, therapy, life, the meaning of existence. If "Man is by nature sinful or ridden by primitive instincts," (Freud) then he must be tamed; if he has in him "good" and "bad," then by natural and supernatural means one must be supported and the other combatted; but if "we believe that inherent in man are evolutionary constructive forces. . . . It means that man, by his very nature and of his own accord, strives toward self-realization, that his set of values evolves from such striving. . . . We arrive thus at a *morality of evolution,* in which . . . to work at ourselves becomes not only the prime moral obligation . . . but . . . the prime *moral privilege."*

Horney postulated "The *real self* as that central inner force, common to all human beings and yet unique in each, which is the deep source of growth." It is a dynamic principle, not a thing, a definition of faith and its possible manifestation. With this concept Horney enters those areas of human existence and human endeavor we call religion, ethics and philosophy. The real self is not only a unitary concept, universal to the point of being cosmic, but is also an expression of and an aid to approximating new human ultimates.

It is my feeling that had she lived, Horney's next book

would have reflected a considerable development of the concept of the real self. It could form the basis of the as yet unwritten psychology of human wholeness in health and sickness, and expand our awareness of the meaning and nature of existence. But while *Neurosis and Human Growth* is not a final formulation, it is a brilliant and penetrating synthesis of her clinical experience and her mature thought.

In her last two works, "On Feeling Abused" and "The Paucity of Inner Experiences," which are published for the first time in book form in this volume, Horney extends her discussion of alienation from self. These essays and three of her lectures on technique, which are also included in this volume, add new dimensions to her earlier formulations and chart new directions for research and therapy. For many years Horney talked about "sometime writing a book on technique." But her lectures and papers on technique usually evolved into new elaborations of theory; and "A constantly evolving and changing theory and therapy do not easily lend themselves to technique formulations. Horney regarded therapy as a uniquely human cooperative venture. Anything that suggested dogma or rules, techniques or dehumanization, was contrary to the spirit of her theory, philosophy, and goals in therapy. Holistic psychoanalysis, by its very nature, must conduct its therapy and investigations with the loosest kinds of tentative, though clearly stated, guides to make possible the emergence of the uniquely human." [6]

In briefly summarizing Horney's work and ideas, I have tried to show that she pioneered and extended the frontiers

[6] Kelman, H., "The Holistic Approach (Horney)." In *American Handbook of Psychiatry*, II, ed. S. Arieti, Basic Books, New York, 1959.

of psychoanalysis. But perhaps the best indication of the impact of her personality and ideas can be found in the work of her colleagues who participated with her in the evolution of her theories and since her death have contributed significantly to the advancement of psychoanalysis in its many aspects.

Horney had been criticized for what appeared to be a lack of interest in and emphasis on childhood. In part her failure to do so was in reaction to what she regarded as Freud's one-sided overemphasis. Also her interests were moving in other directions which, in fact, opened childhood to much wider and deeper understanding than was possible with Freud's rigidly deterministic and instinctivistic thinking. In "Character Development in Young Children," Dr. Norman Kelman utilizes Horney's holistic growth-oriented philosophy in understanding and evaluating the *whole* child.

My own "A Unitary Theory of Anxiety" also fits into Horney's evolving ideas. I have attempted to illuminate the distinctions between fear and anxiety in health and sickness, during waking and dreaming. I have also attempted a comprehensive examination of the sources of anxiety, its functions and the attitudes toward it.

In "The Body's Participation in Dilemma and Anxiety Phenomena" Dr. Alexander R. Martin gives a detailed phenomenologic analysis of the processes of denying conflict or admitting it into awareness. Evidence cited, that integration precedes individuation, supports Horney's notion of acquired conflict and her optimistic view of therapy. Dr. Martin shows how repressing conflict leads to physical symptoms, so-called psycho-somatic disorders and certain types of mental illness; but he emphasizes that that anxiety is not caused by conflict but is an expression of the emergent awareness of it.

Horney often was criticized for "the absence of sex" in her theory. But rather than being absent, sex assumes a comprehensive and appropriate place in her theory as an expression of total human involvement. Dr. Frederick A. Weiss elaborates this thesis in "Some Aspects of Sex in Neuroses" and gives a cogent critique of Freud's position "regarding the neuroses as being without exception disturbances of the sexual function." His ideas on the variety of forms of symbiosis enhance our understanding of how interpersonal and intrapsychic factors, negative body image and alienation from self participate in the misuses of sex in sick "love" relationships. His findings underline the value of "the analysis of the total character structure" for a constructive resolution of sexual difficulties.

While Freud understandably started with the notion of the detached observer, he saw the need for the concept of countertransference and later spoke of the educational function of psychoanalysis. Accepting that the therapist does influence the patient, Dr. Muriel Ivimey in "Neurotic Guilt and Healthy Moral Judgment" examines how and toward what ends. She also examines the nature of unproductive and productive guilt feelings and the means of lessening the former so that the increased strength of the latter can enhance opportunities for the patient's spontaneous morality and growth to develop. Her critique of Freud's view of guilt and that of some religions illuminates the central and comprehensive place of morality in Horney's philosophy of theory and therapy.

Self-hate as a neurotic phenomenon and not as an expression of innate self-destructiveness, or of a death instinct, are crucial to Dr. Elizabeth Kilpatrick's "A Psychoanalytic Understanding of Suicide." Again using Horney's holistic approach, Dr. Kilpatrick shows how historical, religious and cultural factors influence the frequency and meaning of suicide and how the constructive forces of the real self participate in therapy. Her delineation of the psychodynamics of this human possibility gives us more detailed and comprehensive guides toward understanding this human tragedy.

Thus Karen Horney's contributions to the understanding of human behavior live on in her own writings, and have been carried forward in the work of her students and colleagues. It is the sincere hope of the contributors that this volume will add to the further understanding and appreciation of her ideas.

HAROLD KELMAN

New York City
1963

ACKNOWLEDGMENTS

This book is sponsored by the Association for the Advancement of Psychoanalysis, and its official organ, *The American Journal of Psychoanalysis*. Acknowledgment and thanks are owed first of all to its many members and contributors. Special thanks are due the members of the committee responsible for the publication of this volume, Doctors Louis De Rosis, Abe Pinsky, Isidore Portnoy and Ralph Slater. They shared the burdens and participated in the numerous difficult decisions that are part of such a project.

THE CONTRIBUTORS

Morton B. Cantor, M.D. St. Louis University 1947; Diplomate, American Board of Neurology and Psychiatry; Fellow, Academy of Psychoanalysis; Lecturer, American Institute for Psychoanalysis; Associate Psychoanalyst, Karen Horney Clinic.

Karen Horney, M.D. University of Berlin 1913; Training Analyst and Lecturer, Berlin Psychoanalytic Institute 1918–32; Associate Director, Chicago Psychoanalytic Institute 1932–34; Training Analyst and Lecturer, New York Psychoanalytic Institute 1934–41; Founding Dean, American Institute for Psychoanalysis; Founding Editor, *The American Journal of Psychoanalysis;* author of *The Neurotic Personality of Our Time* and others; editor of *Are You Considering Psychoanalysis?*

Muriel Ivimey, M.D. Johns Hopkins 1922; Original Member, Training Analyst, Lecturer and Associate Dean, American Institute for Psychoanalysis, until her death in 1953; President, Association for the Advancement of Psychoanalysis.

Harold Kelman, M.D. Harvard 1931; D.Md.Sc. Columbia 1938; Diplomate, American Board of Neurology and Psychiatry; Charter Fellow now Councillor, Academy of

Psychoanalysis; Founding Member, former President, now Dean, American Institute for Psychoanalysis; Editor, *The American Journal of Psychoanalysis.*

Norman Kelman, M.A. Columbia 1937; M.D. Harvard 1941; Assistant Clinical Professor, Yale 1957–; former Associate Dean, now Training Analyst and Lecturer, American Institute for Psychoanalysis; Fellow, Academy of Psychoanalysis.

Elizabeth Kilpatrick, C.M. Dalhousie University 1915; M.D. Long Island College of Medicine 1925; Charter Fellow, Academy of Psychoanalysis; Training Analyst, Lecturer and Dean (1952–54), American Institute for Psychoanalysis; Lecturer in Psychiatry, Dalhousie University 1960–.

Alexander R. Martin, M.B., B.Ch. Queen's University of Belfast 1923; M.D. 1933; Hon. L.L.D. 1962; Diploma in Psychological Medicine, Royal College P.&S., London, 1926; Life Fellow and Former Chairman of the Committee on Leisure Time Activity, A.P.A.; Charter Fellow, Academy of Psychoanalysis; Founding Member and original Training Analyst, American Institute for Psychoanalysis.

Emy A. Metzger, M.D. University of Munich 1923; Diplomate, American Board of Neurology and Psychiatry; Fellow, Academy of Psychoanalysis; formerly Lecturer, American Institute for Psychoanalysis.

Ralph Slater, M.D. New York University 1938; Diplomate, American Board of Neurology and Psychiatry; Fellow, Academy of Psychoanalysis; Lecturer, American Institute for Psychoanalysis; Associate Psychoanalyst, Karen Horney Clinic; Managing Editor, *The American Journal of Psychoanalysis.*

Frederick A. Weiss, M.D. University of Berlin 1926;

Charter Fellow, Academy of Psychoanalysis; Former President, Association for the Advancement of Psychoanalysis; Training Analyst and Lecturer, American Institute for Psychoanalysis.

ADVANCES IN PSYCHOANALYSIS

On Feeling Abused

KAREN HORNEY

When speaking of feeling abused I refer to a neurotic
phenomenon which is well known to psychoanalysts
in all its multiple facets. Patients may dwell on the harm
done to them by previous psychotherapists, by other physicians, by their boss, wife or friends, and, going all the way
back, by their parents. In more diffuse ways, they may also
feel themselves to be victims of social institutions, or of
fate in general.

The particular content of such complaints varies in-
finitely. The emphasis may be on the general iniquity of
fate. The patient may be convinced, then, that everybody
is better off than he. Others find a better job, get a raise
in salary; their clocks always keep the correct time, their
cars never need repairs, their sorrows are negligible. More
specifically, the emphasis may be on injustice done to him.
He, the patient, has been cooperative, efficient, helpful,
understanding; he has, in fact, done more than his share.
But he got an unfair deal. The others failed to be grateful,
to help him, to consider him, or even to show a minimum

Read before the Association for the Advancement of Psychoanalysis
at the New York Academy of Medicine on February 28, 1951. Reprinted from *The American Journal of Psychoanalysis*, XI, 1, 1951.

of decency. The emphasis may be on others' criticizing and accusing him, imputing motivations that were quite alien to him. He may feel exploited and imposed upon. Everybody seems to want something from him, or, indeed, to expect the impossible of him and to make him feel guilty if he does not measure up to their expectations. The emphasis may be on being frustrated by others: "They" frustrate him; they keep him down; they squelch every joy he may have; they put every possible obstacle in the way of his achievements, or of his career. They begrudge every advantage he has, or every step ahead he takes. They humiliate him, slight him, despise him, disregard him. They betray and deceive him. There are but fine transitions from this state to that of the paranoid psychotic who feels spied upon, imperiled, persecuted, or ruined beyond repair.

As the neurotic patient gradually reveals these experiences, we are struck not so much by their kind, but by their frequency and intensity. We all not only *may have,* but in fact *have had* similar experiences. We all have been used as a means to an end. We have been deceived or disappointed. We have without exception had unfortunate human experiences in our early childhood which were painful and have left their traces. In other words, such experiences seem to belong to the human suffering we must bear and accept. And they may help us to become more discerning, more tolerant and to develop more compassion for the suffering of others.

The more entangled by unsolved inner conflicts a person is, the more do these experiences change in quantity and quality. Generally speaking, the main difference is one between external provocation (factual affronts, offenses, etc.) and emotional responses. To begin with, the neurotic

person himself often elicits inconsiderate or offensive treatment by his behavior without being aware of it. He may
be so compulsively compliant, helpful and appeasing that
he inadvertently invites others to run all over him. He
may alienate others by his irritability and arrogance, but
being unaware of his provocative behavior he may experience only that they reject or slight him in an entirely undeserved manner. This factor alone renders the frequency
of factual abuse greater than for the relatively healthy
person.

DISPROPORTIONATE RESPONSES

Furthermore, the patient's emotional responses to factual trespasses or mishaps are quite out of proportion.
Because of his irrational claims, his demands on himself,
his neurotic pride, his self-contempt and his self-accusations, he is so diffusely vulnerable that he is bound to feel
hurt more often and more deeply. Minor occurrences,
such as requests made of him, friends not accepting his
invitation, disagreements with his wishes or opinions, are
experienced as major tragedies.

Finally, even when there is no particular provocation
from the outside, even with his knowing full well that his
life-situation is a favorable one, he nevertheless may feel
abused. He will, then, in subtle and gross ways—unconsciously—distort the actual conditions and give them in his
mind a little twist, so that he appears as the victim, after
all. This observation indicates that feeling abused is not
only a patient's subjective response to existing difficulties
in life. It is, in addition, prompted by some inner necessity
which irresistibly *pulls* him to experience life the way he

does.

The sum total of these factors often makes for a diffuse feeling of abuse. When speaking thus of feeling abused, I mean a person's rather pervasive experience of being the victim—a feeling which in its extent and intensity goes beyond, and is out of proportion to, actual provocations and may become a way of experiencing life.

All these various feelings of being unfairly treated stem from different sources within the individual and must be traced individually. For instance, a neurotic person so easily feels accused by the analyst, or some one else, because he is constantly accusing himself without knowing it; or, at any rate, without knowing the extent and intensity of his self-accusations. Or, he feels easily slighted because his insatiable need for recognition lets anything short of unequivocal agreement or admiration appear to be a slight. He feels coerced so easily by others because he is so little aware of his own wishes or opinions and is relentlessly driven by his own demands on himself. All these individual connections must be traced and worked through in analytical therapy. But it is also important to see the totality of the picture because only by so doing—as we shall see presently—can we recognize the general background of feeling abused or victimized. This is the reason why I shall neglect the individual sources in this paper, and why I lump together under the heading of "Feeling Abused" all experiences of the kind mentioned so far.

UNAWARENESS OF FEELING ABUSED

The *awareness* of feeling abused varies, which in itself is a rather astonishing fact. Whatever the conditions, reasons and functions for feeling abused may be, it always has the one function of making others, or circumstances, responsible for what is wrong in one's own life. This would entail an unconscious interest in emphasizing the fact of being abused, and leads us to expect that the experience as such would always be conscious. This, however, is not generally true because a person may also have strong reasons for not being aware of it. The following three main reasons may militate against awareness.

Since feeling abused always breeds resentment, a person may be afraid of experiencing this resentment and its disrupting effect on human relations, and may therefore tend to keep it from awareness. Thus, the unconscious interest in these instances lies not in suppressing the experience of being abused as such, but in removing reasons for resentment.

In other instances, a pride in invulnerability and in inviolability leads people to suppress the experience. Nothing should happen—and therefore does not happen—that is not initiated by them, or under their control.

A third reason lies in the pride in endurance. They should be so strong—and therefore they *are* so strong— that nothing and nobody can hurt them. They should be able to put up with everything. They should have the unruffled serenity of a Buddha. Conversely, the very feeling of being hurt, injured, humiliated, rejected is a blow to their pride and, hence, tends to be suppressed.

VARIATIONS IN ATTITUDES

The attitudes toward feeling abused, or the emotional responses to such feeling, also vary. People with predominantly self-effacing trends tend to suppress the resulting resentment and develop a more or less concealed pride in suffering under a world which is morally inferior to them. Predominantly aggressive and expansive people, while not owning up to hurt feelings, tend to respond with plain anger, moral indignation and vindictiveness. The predominantly resigned person tends to assume a philosophical, detached attitude toward it. He takes it for granted that people are not to be trusted and withdraws from them.

Notwithstanding these variations in awareness and response, feeling abused has in itself some characteristics which are always present: the abuse is felt as real. It goes with a feeling of being not only the victim, but the innocent victim. It entails the feeling of, "It happens to me."

It feels real. People *are* unfair, ungrateful, condemnatory, demanding, deceitful, and therefore the patient's feeling abused is an entirely rational response. He will dwell on those situations in which realistic harm was done to him, whether in childhood or later on. He tends to maintain this attitude even though he may have recognized in many individual incidents that the vulnerability of his own pride or the externalization of his self-abuse were the incisive factors in bringing about his feeling abused by others. But such isolated insights do little to undermine the whole phenomenon. They still leave him with the feeling that by and large he *is* the victim of others, or of circumstances. In fact, a silent battle goes on between the analyst and the patient on this very score: the analyst stressing the subjective factors; the patient in ever so many versions emphasising the stark reality of the abuse. He may at best admit that his reactions to unfair treatments are exaggerated.

The fact of such a struggle against evidence to the contrary permits the assumption that the patient must have a strong unconscious interest in seeing the sources as outside of, rather than inside, himself.

He is the innocent victim. In more or less articulate or subtle forms, the patient will stress how undeserved are the mishaps which have befallen him. His own virtue and rightness, his purity, his goodness, his fairness appear to him in striking contrast to the deal he receives from others or from fate.

"It happens to me." The patient experiences himself as the passive recipient of wrongs done to him. Passivity in this context does not always mean the emphasis on his helplessness. The expansive "types," as we know, abhor any admission of helplessness. They may be determined to prevent, by their vigilance and their planning, the perpetration of any harm. Or, they may be most active in getting back in a punitive way at anyone injuring them. The general implication of passivity here is rather the person's feeling that the abuses have nothing whatever to do with him, that they hit him like rain-storms, cold or heat. One of the results is that his major energies may be engaged in a battle with outside hostile forces, warding them off, appeasing them or withdrawing from them.

IMPLICATIONS FOR THERAPY

With the therapeutic aim of bringing patients back to themselves, the analyst will try to show them the extent to which their pride, their claims, their self-accusations, their self-contempt, their self-frustration, and so on, are responsible for their experiencing life as we have described it to this point. But these endeavors, although undertaken conscientiously, often meet with difficulties. The complaints may be driven underground, but the patients keep feeling wary, vindictive, appeasing. My contention is that these difficulties are due to an insufficient understanding of the whole phenomenon.

The analyst has no doubt whatever that the individual connections which he uncovers between the subjective factors in the patient and his feeling abused are true. What is more important, neither has the patient any doubts about their validity. But the patient does not *experience* these factors. He may, in fact, not experience much of anything that is going on within himself. He will, for instance, recognize that his feeling frustrated can be but a result of his own pride or irrational claims, or that his feeling disregarded and despised can be but a result of his self-contempt. But as long as he does not *experience* his claims or his self-contempt, these explanations must remain for him probable deductions which, of course, carry hardly any weight. If the analyst mistakes such intellectual agreements for real acceptance, he starts to walk on quicksand with every further step he takes.

The patient may not feel himself at all an active factor in his own life. He lives as though his life were determined by outside forces. While on the one hand there is a paucity of inner experiences, which often shows in a physical feeling of emptiness, or in compulsive hunger, his vision and energies are, on the other hand, all outward bound. While he may be consciously convinced that heaven and hell are within ourselves, this is *not* what he feels and how he lives. On a deeper level of his being, good and evil all seem to come from outside. He expects the solutions to his problem, or his fulfillment, through a change in external factors: through love, through company, success, power, prestige. Having no real feeling for his own value, affirmation of himself can come only by the approval or recognition of others. As long as his interest is thus outward bound, he cannot, despite his best intentions, be interested in his difficulties, but must primarily be interested in what others think of him, or in the ways in which he can manipulate others. It does not matter, in this context, whether this manipulation is being done by charm, appeasement, impression, intimidation, or domination.

LOOKING OUT, NOT IN

Also, as long as he does not experience *his* feelings, *his* thoughts, *his* actions, he cannot possibly feel responsible for himself, or for his life. Whatever difficulties arise can only be brought about by others. "They" keep him down, disregard him, take advantage of him, coerce him. So, energies must be directed outward not only for attaining good, but for warding off evil, or for vindictively getting back at others. It is important for the analyst to realize that the patient may not only externalize this or that inner factor, but that his whole way of living is an *externalized living*. As a patient put it succinctly: "He looks out and not in."

When we understand the whole extent of such externalized living, with all its implications, it then becomes clear that feeling abused is but part and parcel of such living. For therapy this means that we cannot hope to make much headway with analyzing individual incidents of feeling abused before having exposed his externalized living as such.

We must look at the externalized living in two ways. As I have described it, it is a result of a paucity of inner experiences, of the loss of feeling a center of gravity in oneself and the absence of feeling oneself as a determining factor in one's own life. Briefly, it is one of the results of the alienation from self. But it is not only a result. It also acquires a function. It becomes an effective means for preventing a person from ever facing his problems, or even from being interested in them. Externalizing living, in other words, becomes a *centrifugal* living, characterized by active and often frantic moves away from self. The more a person emphasizes in his own mind the reality of others' unfairness, impositions, or cruelty, the more effectively can he evade facing his own vulnerability, the tyranny of his own demands on himself, the relentlessness of his self-abuse; the more the responsibility for self becomes meaningless in his mind.

In this sense, feeling abused becomes an over-all defense against owning up to any neurotic drive or conflict within himself.

This is the reason why he not only experiences himself as the victim, but feels irresistibly pulled in this direction. In other words, he not only feels easily humiliated because of many factors in his inner constellation, but he has a definite unconscious interest in emphasizing and exaggerating such "humiliations." This is why the patient's feeling abused is such an intricate mixture of facts and fancy. There is factual abuse, invited or uninvited. And there is abuse fabricated out of thin air, which seems as real to the person suffering it as the table he can grasp with his hands. It may create intense suffering, out of proportion to the provocation—and may barely touch the conscious mind, although it will be stored in deeper layers. Modifying Voltaire's words on the existence of God: if there were no abuse, the patient would have to invent it.

In certain phases of analytical therapy we can observe and uncover rapidly this defense function of feeling abused. But after the tendency has subsided to some extent, it may suddenly re-emerge with an impact brushing aside all reason. The patient may bring forth one association after the other, concerning the wrongs done to him, or he may be suddenly swept away by a huge wave of vindictiveness produced by a massive feeling of abuse. All of these complaints or rages, then, can be readily dispelled by the simple question: "Have you not come close to facing a problem in yourself, and are you not trying to ward off its realization?"

DEFENSE AGAINST RECOGNITION

Patients who are familiar with this defense function may themselves catch on quickly to any emergence of feeling abused. Instead of wasting much time justifying the reproaches felt against others, they may take them as a signal, indicating their need to avoid a realization of some emerging problem of their own. Conversely, as long as the patient has not yet recognized this defense function, he will bitterly resent as an unfair imposition any suggestion of self-scrutiny. He is the one who is harassed by his boss, his wife, his friends, so why should he, in addition to all the wrong done to him, go through the humiliating process of self-examination and change? This is a reaction which again demonstrates his intrinsic lack of interest in outgrowing his difficulties. He may not be able, however, to experience and express this response of resentment to the analyst and the whole analytic procedure. But under the stress of having to be rational and having to appease, he may cover it up with a polite intellectual interest in the analyst's suggestions. The inevitable result is that nothing sinks in and nothing changes!

When, thus, we see feeling abused as an expression of centrifugal living and as a patient's over-all defense against facing his own problems and assuming responsibility for them, the phenomenon assumes a crucial importance in the neurotic process and in analytical therapy. It is, indeed, one of the main factors in perpetuating neurotic attitudes. It is like a heavy iron door that blocks access to the recognition of inner problems. But when analyzed sufficiently, it is also a gateway making possible an approach to them.

Does analysis of feeling abused, as described above, help immediately? In some ways its therapeutic effect is visibly beneficial. It does improve the patient's human relationships. He can relate himself better to others, to the extent that he realizes they cannot possibly give him what only he himself can do, and that he cannot make them responsible for things which are his responsibility alone.

In that he feels himself the responsible agency in his life, his feeling of "I" also becomes stronger. Even though owning up to his difficulties is painful, he nevertheless gains a greater feeling of solidity and aliveness. And since he is less preoccupied with what others are, do, or don't do, he can direct more interest and energies toward himself and use them for constructive self-examination.

EXPERIENCING DIFFICULTIES

On the other hand, the very process of coming closer to himself entails being in for a troublesome and upsetting time. It would give a wrong impression if one were to say that he starts only now to see his difficulties. He has already seen many of them. But he saw them, as it were, as possibilities, as assumptions—likely to be, but not really, pertinent to his life. Now he begins to *experience* them and this sets going all his still-existing needs to justify or condemn them, with the result that he feels more divided than he did before. This inner battle can subside only gradually, as his interest in how he *is* increases and his focus on how he *should* be dwindles. At the same time, his real self emerges and he has to defend it against the onslaught of the pride system. All of this means that the symptomatic picture may be temporarily impaired. In simple terms, the patient may at times feel worse than before. Nevertheless, these upsets are constructive because of their being expressive of moves in a constructive direction, a direction toward finding himself and toward self-realization.

If, conversely, feeling abused is not sufficiently analysed, the therapeutic process is bound to suffer. Though the patient may make efforts to get at his problems, these efforts are bound to be half-hearted. Briefly, we could say that nobody can find himself if he keeps running away from himself. The patient cannot possibly be interested in himself and his difficulties as long as—consciously or unconsciously—he makes outside factors responsible for them. He will use whatever superficial insights he gets about himself, to understand, manipulate or change *others*. In addition, he is bound to resent, unconsciously, that he should be the one to change, since, as he experiences it, the others are the ones who make life difficult for him. The analysis thus is bound to be delayed and to move in circles until the analyst wakes up to the fact that the changes which may take place in the patient lag considerably behind the efforts put in because some invisible forces prevent insights from taking root. Going after these invisible forces, he still may be able to get at their sources, but much precious time is lost.

Or, the analysand may have gained sufficient insight into certain aspects of himself, particularly in his relations to others, to function more smoothly. In that case, the analysis may peter out when the patient's obvious troubles are diminished. The patient may feel quite satisfied with what the analysis has done for him and decide to terminate it. His incentive to come to terms with himself for the sake of a more productive life is not great enough when he no longer feels driven by the whip of manifest disturbances.

RISE OF SELF-HATE

Finally, the patient's destructiveness may get out of hand. He may take a definite turn for the worse by becoming both more openly vindictive against others and more self-destructive. The greater vindictiveness against others cannot be explained simply by the patient's increasing freedom to feel and express it. The main danger precipitating such an unfortunate outcome lies in a rise of self-hate, often barely perceptible, but steady and relentless. For quite some time the analysis seems to go on satisfactorily. The patient seems to gain more and more insight into his neurotic structure. He also seems to be better able to cope with many situations. The analyst feels, nevertheless, on precarious grounds. The patient seems eager to learn a few things about himself, but his insights lack depth. He does not follow up on his own any connections he has grasped. His emotional life seems to remain rather barren. His relation to the analyst does not gain in solidity and his tendency to externalize abates but little, though he may be more cautious about expressing it. The patient keeps feeling interpretations as accusations and tends to justify himself automatically.

Among the factors the patient has seen within himself are also some of the sources of feeling abused: his pride, his irrational claims, his fear of self-reproaches and the subsequent tendency to put the blame on others, his need to use the others as scapegoats for his not measuring up to the height of his inner dictates. And with such realizations, the feeling abused, too, seems to recede.

EXTERNALIZING SELF-ABUSE

But as the analysis goes on, the patient's defenses start to wear thin and some of his problems begin to hit home. He begins to realize that his having problems is not merely a construct, but an existing fact, and he responds to such growing realization with an equally growing self-hate in one form or another—self-condemnation, self-contempt, self-destructiveness. This process, though painful, is not dangerous if the patient has developed sufficient constructive self-interest to help him to retain a healthy perspective on the onslaught of self-hate. If, however, such interest has not developed, he then has nothing to set against the impact of self-hate, and he feels threatened with total collapse or total disintegration. At this point, that part of feeling abused which is, briefly, an externalization of self-abuse comes into the foreground. He may turn against others—including, of course, the analyst—with a more or less

violent vindictiveness. This process which has been described as a simple and rather mechanical "turning outward of aggression" is a desperate attempt on the part of
the patient to make the others—and not himself—appear
as the evil ones. They—and not he—deserve every im-
aginable punishment, defeat and destruction. He is, however, usually not successful in his effort to ward off self-
hate, but on the contrary, is caught in a vicious circle. His
greater vindictiveness against others is likely to increase
the very self-hate he is so anxious to tune down. The resulting inner turmoil makes him panicky and he may break
up the analysis in a state of panic. Even at this stage, if
it is not so far advanced that the patient is inaccessible,
the analyst has still a chance to save the situation, provided
he is alert to the impairment of the patient's relation to
himself and to a rise of the patient's vindictiveness in general. In tackling it, the analyst must be extremely careful
to avoid anything that might feel to the patient like an
accusation. The best way to do so is not to take it at its
face-value, i.e. as retaliatory hostility, but as an expression
of inner distress, caused ultimately by his externalized
living. If, on the other hand, self-hate and vindictiveness
rise to an unbearable degree, the dangers of psychotic episodes or attempts at suicide are fairly great.

ROLE IN THERAPY

Feeling abused plays a more crucial role in therapy than
is usually assumed. Even if the phenomenon is not obvious,
it is important for the analyst to be alert to any signs of
it, particularly in any case of a pervasive tendency to ex-

ternalize; or even more generally, in any case of a dearth of inner experiences because of externalized and centrifugal living. It remains necessary—at the appropriate time—to trace all the individual connections with intra-psychic factors. The analyst must be aware, however, that these connections cannot mean much to the patient as long as he has shut himself off from his inner experiences. As long as he does not feel them, the whole realm of inner experiences remains to him uncanny, weird, mysterious. A too early unravelling of intra-psychic factors, therefore, is a waste of time. When the feeling of abuse is sighted, the analyst must proceed from there to lay bare all the aspects of externalized living, i.e., the ways in which the patient lives for, through and against others. The therapeutic effect of this step is a lessening alienation from self. As the patient gradually realizes how his feeling of his own value, his hopes, concerns, fears, resentments and activities are determined by others, or by factors outside himself, he begins to wonder where *he* is. He wonders how little he *is* in his own life, how little he is the captain of his ship. This wondering is the beginning of an interest in himself and a search for himself.

SUMMARY

To summarize with regard to the phenomenon of feeling abused, it is important to see both the *diversity* of content, form and individual sources, and the *unity* behind such diversity. This unity comes into clear focus only when we lump together all the manifold expressions of feeling abused, and disregard for a while their particular sources in the neurotic structure. Only when seeing the phenom-enon as a whole do we realize that it is an integral part of a whole way of living one's life outside oneself. Only then do we realize that it is a person's over-all defense against coming face to face with himself and his own problems.

The Paucity of Inner Experiences

KAREN HORNEY

All of us have an interest in not being aware of certain
feelings, drives, conflicts, qualities within ourselves.
The particular content of such unconscious factors depends upon the whole personality structure. A person, for
instance, who persistently keeps himself down is unconsciously interested in being unaware of his assets; a person
who needs to keep others at a distance is unconsciously
interested in being unaware of his need for affection.
Briefly, this is one of the basic tenets with which we work
in psychoanalytic therapy. The paucity of inner experiences to be discussed here is a more pervasive haziness of all,
or most, inner experiences. The entire threshold of awareness is lowered.

Neither is the paucity of inner experiences restricted to
the emotional life—feelings of pain, of joy, of hope, of
disappointment, of likes or dislikes. It also includes thinking, willing, wishing, believing, doing. In short, it means
living in a fog.

It is not identical with an alienation from the real self,

Read before the Association for the Advancement of Psychoanalysis
at the New York Academy of Medicine on February 27, 1952. Reprinted from *The American Journal of Psychoanalysis,* XII, 1, 1952.

but concerns the whole actual self: the awareness of pride and self-hate, triumph and defeat, hurts, illusions. Even anger, though unmistakably shown, may not be felt as such.

One last point to define the nature of the problem: the world of inner experiences is not shrivelled or extinct. Dreams that the memory retains are like the rumblings of distant volcanos or thunderstorms and reflect the depth and aliveness of inner battles, of destruction, of despair, of attempts at some solution. But this inner world is not accessible to conscious experience. We can describe the condition by analogies only, analogies which are artificially constructed, but are taken from symbols as they may appear in dreams. It is as if the person had turned his back on his inner life; as if it all was covered by fog; as if he had closed an airtight or soundproof door; as if he had walled off everything. It may be a glass wall through which he still can observe what is going on without experiencing it. The fog is usually not always equally thick; it may lift at times and at others become impenetrable. Then feelings of unreality may result. All of a sudden some hurts, some loss, some work of art may penetrate and elicit a response. Some areas may be relatively free, like a relation to nature or music.

The problem can be tackled from various angles, such as its genesis and development in the individual, or its role in the neurotic process. I want to focus on the questions which have a rather direct bearing on therapy: the manifestations by which to recognize it; its influence on life and on therapy; the patient's awareness of it and his attitude toward it, and ways in which to tackle it.

Though inconspicuous and, as it were, undramatic, the paucity of inner experiences is a fairly crucial neurotic phenomenon. It is crucial both in the sense that many currents converge to create it and also, that in turn it gives rise to or reinforces several neurotic disturbances. The currents which contribute to its formation are of a general nature, inherent in every neurotic process. Hence the dearth of inner experience itself also is not restricted to any special kind of neurotic development, which means it seems to occur independently of so-called types.

The subsequent disturbances, manifold as they are, in principle can be put into two categories. One of these categories can be understood as that of substitute-functions. The unawareness of inner experiences is after all a severe deficiency. Not only does it impair a person's aliveness but also his functioning in daily life. It is to be compared perhaps with the loss of eyesight, jeopardizing his orientation. One might even call it a kind of inner blindness. This analogy allows for a further step. If somebody becomes blind, he will find other ways to orient himself in his surroundings. The person who is numbed to his inner experiences likewise must find other ways, and he does so automatically. The most important one is to shift emphasis from the inner to the outer life. Ordinarily we do not care to make much of a distinction between the inner and outer life, because they are indeed an interwoven texture. But just as the inner life comes into full focus when attention is withdrawn from externals—as in meditating or dreaming—so, conversely, externals dominate the picture when the inner life is dimmed out. If such one-sided emphasis on externals is rather pervasive, we speak of "externalized living." [1,2]

NATURE OF EXTERNALIZED LIVING

Roughly, that entails the following characteristics: intra-psychic processes are experienced as interpersonal ones. For instance, a person does not feel that he despises himself, but he is aware of despising others, or being despised by them. His own wishes and his own compulsive demands on himself fade out and are replaced by the real or imagined expectations of others. The expectations of others, then, have the same compulsory character as his own "shoulds," i.e., he must meet them or rebel against them. He is what others think of him; prestige or success may become the only measuring rods for his value. In conjunction with such delegating of his rights to others, the emphasis shifts from *being* to *appearing*. What counts then is proper be-havior, proper functioning, physical looks—in short, the role he plays or the impression he makes on others. A feel-ing of anxiety, for instance, becomes alarming only if it shows in perspiring or in trembling of the hands. In moral terms, this shift from being to appearing means that he can do anything—lie, steal, cheat, be promiscuous—provided he "gets by" with it. Vigilant observation of others becomes a supreme necessity and is cherished as a precious asset.

If a person is aware of his feelings, wishes, fears, beliefs and ideals he is provided with an orientation for his per-sonal life. If all these inner experiences are dimmed out he has, as it were, no directive. The expectations of others or, in a more general way, any kind of rules, regulations or routines supply him with substitute means of orientation. He clings rigidly to these directives and feels lost, anxious or irritable if they are not available. He may be apprehensive, for instance, in any situation when he does not know what is expected of him.

FROM BEING TO THINKING

Another shift of functions—likewise of far-reaching importance—is that from *being* to *thinking*. To speak in terms of Zen Buddhism: "Life is not a problem to be solved but an experience to be realized." The more remote a person is from his inner life, the more abstract his thinking. The less alive he is, the more he may turn into a thinking machine. The more he is cut off from a spontaneous contact with the world around him, the more the subjectivity of his thoughts becomes self-evident truth. The greater his need for superiority (for whatever reasons) the more imperative the necessity of foresight and omniscience.

Not only the faculty of thinking but also that of willing may assume as it were a life of its own. Separate from the context and the reality of the whole living person, it may soar into the fantastic and turn into sheer magic. The belief in the omnipotence of the mind or in its magic powers stems from other sources, but it is perpetuated and reinforced by the unavailability of inner experiences.

The other category of subsequent disturbances is constituted by reactive anxieties. The unawareness of inner experiences gives a person a feeling of emptiness or nothingness which in itself may or may not be conscious. But whether this feeling is conscious or not, it is in any case frightening. On the grounds of our clinical experiences we can understand those philosophers who contend that anxiety ultimately *is* the fear of nothingness (Kierkegaard) or the fear of non-being (Tillich). Though I am not prepared to regard it as the only and ultimate source of anxiety, it is at any rate one of the deep and essential wells from which anxiety springs. This dread of nothingness may appear in rather direct forms, such as a gnawing and painful feeling of bodily emptiness; as a pervasive feeling of the futility and boredom of life; as dread of darkness and aloneness; in nightmarish dreams such as being terror-stricken by seeing a light on an empty bed or becoming blind with terror about being in an empty and dark cave. More often this dread does not appear as such but shows in the attempts to run away from it. There are many ways to do so, such as compulsive and hectic activities to prohibit any breathing spell in which a feeling of futility could make itself felt; compulsive avoidance of ever being alone; compulsive eating or drinking. Blind destructiveness may ensue when a person becomes aware of the futility of life.[3]

FACTORS OF AWARENESS

The *awareness* of such impoverishment varies and depends upon the following factors. To begin with a rather self-evident fact, a person can miss his own depth only if ever—even for a short period in the past—he has been alive and alert; he may, for instance, in his teens have played with heart and soul at some sport, enjoyed dramatics, or politics; he may have gone through a turbulent time with his first love affair, and his emotional deadness may have set in after such periods. Hence he knows by contrast the difference between a meaningful life and an empty one. Speaking of the present, even a fairly healthy individual is not always equally alive. He, too, knows by contrast when the beauty of a tree merely registers or is actually felt as such; when he is productive or merely works under pressure. The same holds true for many less healthy people. Here the times of aliveness are more rare, and they are more often tied up to conditions of questionable value such as the thrill of conquest, power, triumph, sadistic pursuits.

Furthermore, a person's awareness of his feeling of inner emptiness depends upon the extent of his success in running away from it. He may have such a multitude of social contacts, so many committees to attend, so many "friends," so many cocktail parties, so much shopping or house cleaning, such an amount of business to attend to, that he remains unaware of how meaningless everything is to him.

Finally, we have to consider whether a person is consciously or mostly unconsciously interested in being aware or unaware of the paucity of inner experiences. (The question of the unconscious interest is crucial in *any* attempt to account for awareness or unawareness of *any* factor; the interest being determined by the whole inner constellation.) Does he want to be alive, or is he afraid of it? Is he proud of deep feelings or convictions; or is he proud of being above wants, needs, passions, beliefs. In the latter case he would speak of being "unsentimental," "unemotional," "impassionate," "poised," "stoical," "detached," "objective," "impersonal."

The suffering that may be entailed in the inner retrenchment—leaving out the subsequent anxieties—is as undramatic as the phenomenon itself: a more or less vague feeling of missing out on something, of yearning or discontentment. Although we can understand the reasons for this relative unconcern, we may, nevertheless, from a broader perspective wonder about it, because the disturbance strikes at the very root of our existence. It means, after all, non-living, missing out—not on this or that factor, like success or sex or material assets—but on life itself. Whatever he does or gains, good, bad or indifferent, life passes him by, he is excluded from it.

RESULTANT PROBLEMS

In psychoanalytic therapy the paucity of inner experiences essentially makes for two main difficulties, the combination of which amounts to a severe impasse. On the one hand, as long as the condition persists, in its turn it perpetuates many neurotic processes, some of which were mentioned as substitute phenomena. It means for therapy that the patient keeps externalizing and intellectualizing; that he keeps expecting to solve his difficulties by knowing the reason why they exist, i.e., by looking at them and talking about them; often enough by looking at the difficulties of others and talking about these. He insists on overcoming his difficulties by sheer willpower from one day to the other, or depends upon the analyst having the magic key to set him free. He keeps running away from his feeling of inner emptiness.

On the other hand, the very wall that separates him from his inner experiences also prevents any insight from penetrating this wall. We are more and more convinced that in therapy only that counts which is felt and experienced. Realizing something intellectually is merely the first step and without much therapeutic value if it does not stir up some emotional response. The patient must feel his conflicts,[4] live with his self-contempt, experience how unrelated he is to anything. As long as the patient remains remote from himself, he may now and then have a short-lived emotional response, but closes up soon after. He may talk about a problem intelligently, glibly or even enthusiastically—which is very deceptive—but his apparent interest peters out quickly. In the next hour he may have forgotten all about it, although he may have made conscious efforts to retain the content in his memory. It is like the well-known sensation of a dream vanishing, no matter how hard the dreamer tries to keep it in awareness. He then may pick up another thread, and the same sequence of rising interest and fading out occurs. This results in the analysis easily becoming disconnected and repetitious. Some superficial improvements may take place, but the changes that occur are entirely incommensurate with work put in.

RECOGNIZING THE BLOCKAGE

Naturally, it is important to recognize the condition and the blockage it represents to therapeutic progress. This is not always easy, because the picture may be obscured by the patient's intellectual eagerness and the intellectual grasp of his problems. It is often difficult indeed to distinguish in any direct way what the patient realizes by dint of an intellectual vision—often quite accurate and productive—and what he experiences emotionally. But there are many signs which point indirectly to the nature of the blockage. The safest of these is the petering out of interest in whatever problem emerges. Besides, there are all the disturbances which in some way or other are connected with the condition, like pervasive and tenacious externalizations, compulsive eating, incapacity to be alone, etc. Finally there are dreams which unmistakably may depict inner emptiness or emotional deadness: dreams of marble statues, corpses, empty frames, empty rooms, loss of identity and the nightmares mentioned before.

TACKLING THE PROBLEM

An early recognition of the blockage gives the analyst a vision of the odds against which the analytical work will have to militate, odds which at first sight look like an impasse because the very paucity of inner experiences that keeps neurotic processes going also keeps him from reaching the patient. Such recognition prevents the analyst from getting bewildered and discouraged as the analysis goes on, or from deceiving himself about seeming progress. Nevertheless, an early recognition is of no immediate help. He cannot possibly confront the patient with his feelings of nothingness as long as he has nothing to fall back on. The analyst's first aim, therefore, is to help the patient toward some measure of self-knowledge, toward some measure of inner relatedness to himself. He will tackle whatever is available of his neurotic structure, like various kinds of power drives in an expansive person, or aspects of self-doubts, self-berating or appeasing in a self-effacing type.

Though insights thus gained are on an intellectual level only, they nevertheless help the patient to recognize certain outlines of his structure, or to get a notion of forces operating within him. Even in this initial work it is advisable to make attempts to convey to the patient the distinction between intellectual interest and emotional grasp, between talking from the top of his head and from the bottom of his heart. Perhaps it boils down to the distinction between glibness and sincerity.

The patient who thus has gained some inner strength and some solid ground on which to stand is then ready to be confronted with his feeling of inner emptiness. When he shows in his associations or his dreams signs of interest in the problem, it is profitable for him to become aware of how great this feeling of futility or meaninglessness toward life actually is. His reactions may be more on the positive side, which means that he feels and expresses a longing to come to life, or his prevailing mood may be a defensive one. Pursuing the latter, we realize sooner or later that it is prompted by two kinds of dreads: the dread of the very emptiness itself and the dread of coming to life. These fears are present even though the particular patient may have complained bitterly about his emotional deadness. In any case the patient's feelings are different from the analyst's. The analyst is convinced that a merely perfunctory living is altogether undesirable, that it means vegetating instead of living, that it is altogether desirable to be alive in one's inner experiences. The patient has at best divided feelings. The prospect of greater aliveness is more or less appealing, though because of his dreads he may consciously adopt a "don't care" attitude. But on the other hand, he is reluctant or averse to taking any steps leading toward this direction.

The next objective thus becomes to examine the nature of the dreads. One of them is the dread of *facing* his feeling of nothingness, instead of running away from it. It is to the credit of Dr. Ralph Harris to have first seen the therapeutic importance of this step. As in so many steps leading to some decisive discoveries, the underlying idea here was perfectly simple: apparently nothing can happen as long as the patient finds sufficient means to avoid the issue. If, however—and only if—he fully experiences his feeling of emptiness, then the possibility opens up for something constructive growing out of such a step. The aspect of this problem which is accessible to him varies. To some patients, for instance, the word "emptiness" does not mean much, but the words "futility" or "unrelatedness" do. The process goes from fleeting, vague or localized feelings of futility to a clear or comprehensive experience of how little meaning all or most aspects of life have for him. He may have had doubts before of whether he was really interested in his work; or he may have been concerned about feeling bored so easily, or about short-lived enthusiasms leaving him flat and empty. Now he begins to feel that at bottom he is not related to anything. Such experience, naturally, is terrifying. It feels like life evaporating, like losing the ground under his feet, like being lost in a fog of nothingness.

PENETRATING THE WALL

But such experience, coming at a time when a patient is ready for it, has a constructive effect. Somehow it has the power to penetrate through the wall to his alive core; he feels closer to himself. To put it differently, he begins to realize feelingly that his emptiness is not a plain, unalterable fact, but that there is an alive core of himself that wants to live and that reaches out for a meaning. Several factors account for such a fact. In intellectual terms I would say that one must first recognize the spurious or tenuous nature of one's relatedness to things and people before something real and genuine can grow. Such a description, however, is inadequate for the simple reason that this is not an intellectual process. Probably we come closer to the truth when we consider that a person's experience of emptiness or unrelatedness is so contrary to the meaning of life that it elicits a countermove of a positive nature.

To illustrate this process with an experience of a different kind: during a difficult period of his life, a patient had incurred a near-fatal accident. Soon after this event he almost succumbed to an acute organic disease. Then a friend of his, who knew about his precarious life situation and felt worried about his nearly dying twice in a brief period, said to him: "Why do you want to die?" The patient contended that this question actually saved his life. Because in a flash he feelingly recognized that he wanted to die, indeed. And it was the recognition of this danger that mobilized his will to live.

Perhaps our view of such experiences will be clearer when we compare it with the view J. P. Sartre has expressed in his writings. Sartre likewise stresses the importance of facing nothingness. He also is aware of such a step requiring greater than average courage. But he does not see the feeling of emptiness as the outcome of a neurotic process. In his opinion life *is* meaningless, and it is better to do away with illusions about it and avoid their inevitable repercussions by facing the fact of its futility.

FEAR OF LIFE

The second major dread that counteracts the patient's emerging wish to overcome his emotional deadness concerns the prospect of coming to life. This dread is clearly illustrated by a patient's dream of a vegetable coming to life and his feeling terrified at this sight. This dream occurred at a time when the patient started to realize the meaninglessness of his life; it was a condensed expression of his life; it was a condensed expression of the realization of his wish to come to life. In this dream he explicitly takes a stand by calling his present way of living a mere vegetating. In a condensed form he expresses both his wish to come to life and his dread of it.

In order to understand this dread we must consider that the general lowering of awareness has important functions. It keeps a person from recognizing contradictions, discrepancies and pretenses in his personality, or, generally speaking, from recognizing an existing disorder. It makes it possible not to let his left hand know what his right hand does. He may remain unaware, for instance, that his actions toward employees are contrary to his fine social sentiments, or that his amiability is artificial and not in accord with his using people as steppingstones toward his own glory, etc. In short, unawareness protects illusions and unconscious pretenses.

Furthermore, it is an over-all protection against all *painful* inner experiences. Scrutinizing the nature of these painful experiences, we will be inclined to focus on this or that particular factor. Not only may we do so with different patients, but also during various periods of *one* analysis. It often looks as though the patient was "really" running away from experiencing his conflicts, or his self-hate, or his failure to measure up to his demands, or his claims and their frustrations. Actually he avoids *all* of these experiences. Even this comprehensive answer is not yet fully satisfactory because there are after all many patients who at the proper time are capable of experiencing their conflicts, their self-contempt, etc. Therefore, we must seek the reason that renders such experience unbearable.

The patients of whom I am talking harbor an uncon-

scious but firmly entrenched belief in their omnipotence
and omniscience. While such belief is inherent in every
neurosis its intensity varies. Leaving out its individual
development, there seems to be a correlation between the
paucity of inner experiences on the one hand, and an unconscious reliance upon unlimited powers of the mind on
the other. The more removed a person is from his inner
experiences, the more rigidly does he adhere to the belief
in his omnipotence, the more this belief becomes a vicarious source of strength—yes, a vicarious ground on which
to live. It would need more observations to see whether or
not this correlation is a regular one. I can only say at this
point that it seems plausible and that I have not yet seen
one exception.

The reverse side of this belief in omnipotence is a profound dread of anything connoting helplessness. Any experience of helplessness is not only felt like utter disgrace
and humiliation, but like an earthquake shattering the very
ground on which he stands.

VALUE OF UNAWARENESS

Let us consider now the influence which this whole problem of omnipotence-helplessness has on the patient's experiencing his difficulties in analysis. To feel any force in
himself that is compulsive means that—far from being all-
powerful—he is not even master in his own house. But to
come to life would include feeling in his blood and bones
the grip some compulsive drive has on him.

It is a disgraceful admission of "weakness" that he cannot dispel any difficulty as soon as he recognizes it as such,
by the magic wand of knowledge and will power. To ac-

cept himself with his "failures" would expose him to a shattering experience of impotence. Similarly, he must avoid facing his claims as irrational demands upon the world around him. If he would experience them for what they are, he would be in the ludicrous position of a person clamoring for rights and privileges without any power to enforce them.

To experience a conflict, any conflict—which is painful anyhow—becomes unbearable because it conjures up the humiliating prospect of having to stoop down to make a choice. Moreover, since most neurotic conflicts cannot even be solved by making a choice, the emotional participation in a conflict means the dreaded experience of being helplessly caught in a dilemma from which he cannot extricate himself by magic or violence.

It is this specter of ridicule, disgrace and impotence that accounts for the patient's stringent interest in maintaining a cloak of unawareness. As long as he is not willing or able to relinquish the belief in his magic powers, his budding and growing wish to come to life will be checked by this dread of impotence. And for quite a while the yearning for life and the fight to maintain the belief in omnipotence may alternatively have the upper hand.

RETREAT FROM LIFE

Whenever there is a lurking dread of some inner danger many means are automatically resorted to which would keep such anxiety from emerging, or allay it in case it emerges. The general lowering of awareness is the most pervasive protection in this regard. The most crippling one is a retreat from realistic activity. It proceeds along the principle: "If you don't try, you won't fail." This retreat corresponds to an even more insidious inner restriction which is a consistent tendency to keep oneself down; to develop, as it were, pervasive taboos against any expansive desires both healthy and neurotic. It entails unconsciously cultivating the feeling of "I can't," "I have no rights," "I don't care." Such attitudes may look like abdicating omnipotence, but they actually help to preserve it. They prevent a person from testing his belief in omnipotence and omniscience and thereby allow him to retain it.

The way out of this impasse in principle is the same as the one that leads away from the dread of emptiness. Nothing is gained, nothing can happen as long as we run away from an inner ordeal. The belief in omnipotence and the havoc it causes goes on and on under cover. The patient must experience all that has registered in him as humiliation, disgrace, impotence. He must experience his humiliation of not being the master over life and death; of being subject to laws of cause and effect; of harboring unwarranted fears of so many people or things; of not understanding everything at first glance; of having "to put up with" imperfect people and so on and so forth. He must experience his willing the impossible. He must feelingly realize that he has beaten his head against the stone wall of the impossible. Then, as he accepts the confines of his limitations as a human being, he also can gradually accept and experience himself as he is. The wall between him and his inner life wears down. To put it in terms of Kierkegaard: it seems that *only if we do no longer will the impossible do we have a glimpse of the possible*—which gives us a sense of inner freedom. It seems that caught in the wheels of neurotic processes we have to go through the purgatory of experiencing our inner dreads in order to find the path toward freedom and inner growth.

REFERENCES

1. Horney, K., "On Feeling Abused," this volume, pp. 29–46.
2. Kelman, N., "Clinical Aspects of Externalized Living," *The American Journal of Psychoanalysis*, XII, 1, 1952.
3. Cf. the play of the Swiss author Max Frisch, "Graf Oederland."
4. Martin, A. R., "The Body's Participation in Anxiety and Dilemma Phenomena," this volume, pp. 133–157.

Character Development in Young Children

What are the essential interpersonal relations surrounding the child that assist growth, and what are
the essentials in the nature of the child that make his growing dependent on the outside?

PERSONAL AND FUNCTIONAL RELATIONS

The generalization has been made that the child needs
an atmosphere of love and security in which to develop.
MacMurray [1] specifies this in distinguishing two kinds of
human relationships—the functional and the personal. The
personal relationship is one that has no purpose beyond
itself. Its value comes from the joy each takes in the other
when each brings his whole self to the relationship. A functional relationship is one which has a purpose other than
personal. It exists for the purpose of some deed or project,
like that occupying a doctor and patient, or members of

Read before the Association for the Advancement of Psychoanalysis
at the New York Academy of Medicine on March 22, 1950. Reprinted
from *The American Journal of Psychoanalysis*, X, 1, 1950.

an organization. Such relationships may have personal aspects and be valuable human experiences. When neurotic values are involved, however, an apparently personal relationship may have many ulterior purposes, none of which moves in a constructive direction.

In a child-parent relationship, the atmosphere is healthiest when it is most personal. Often, however, what seems to be a very personal relationship turns out to be merely a functional one. The child's parts, or his functions, receive more attention than his whole being. While the functions of eating and eliminating are prominent in the infant, all too frequently they become the consuming passion of the parents. As parents, what are we out for? Do we want a child who is toilet trained before someone else's child? A child who does not waken when once tucked away? A fine baby diary and photo album? Or are we out for an alive, curious, seeking, exploring, whole child whose spontaneity is a value, whose knowledge is given its place, whose face may be dirty but wreathed by a broad grin, whose knees may be scraped but who discovers for himself what is lurking behind the sofa? It does a child little good if his first step is the signal for a photograph but not for the freedom to use this capacity for his own purposes. If others commandeer him to serve their needs, he will soon be a bundle of parts with little desire for self-realization.

René Spitz[2] and Margaret Ribble[3] describe extreme cases of attending only to the basic, physical needs of the child. Children studied by Spitz in foundling homes, where human contact was minimal, gave striking evidence of psychopathology and lowered vitality. They were extremely susceptible to infection and suffered an exceedingly high mortality rate. Walking, talking, and physical agility were retarded. Emotional reactivity ranged from apathy to violent anxiety. Even in less stark environments, the extent to which an infant's wholeness is subordinated to concern for part functions will effect a dampening of his essential aliveness.

THE GROWING PROCESS

The second basic question involves the essentials in the nature of the child that make his growing dependent on the outside. Growing is a process of integrating increasing capacities, functions, experiences. Dr. Marie Rasey [4] says that growing is the process of becoming more perfectly what one already is. The real self is not a substance that a person has more or less of, but that part of a person that can and wants to grow. In these terms, the child has not less selfness than an adult, but he has less richness and variety which affects the quality of his integrating. Experiences that cause wide fluctuations in the physiology and behavior of the young child barely disturb the integration of an older person. Slight variations in nutrition may alter the stool, the onset of dentition may provoke restlessness, delay in feeding may prompt loud crying and a marked increase in tension.

The child grows and adds to his equipment in two important ways. He increases the effectiveness of what is man's most distinctive possession—his mind. With it, he learns to retain experience and adds the dimension of time to life. He has more possibilities for actualizing, more resources for attempts at a solution of tension.

The infant has the following possibilities for acting on his own behalf: he may cry or make movements that are attention-getting. His responses to needs that are not satisfied take the form of intestinal tract upsets, diarrhea, vomiting, etc., crying, or withdrawal. The consequence of an environment hostile to his needs is a diminished vitality and a narrowing of his possibilities to the point of somnolence, marasmus, hospitalism.

The older infant begins to distinguish people. He differentiates those who satisfy his needs from those who do not. The infant who is nursed will become quiet when taken up by the mother, not by the father. He will start to suck with the mother. If he has an intense need, however, his discrimination may fail him, and sucking may begin with whoever takes him up.

Later, the child develops motility and is able not only to crawl toward the need-satisfier, but also to use other capacities. But when the need is overwhelming, he may lose the use of the new faculty for acting on his own behalf.

An 18-month-old child is able to grasp, walk, call—in short, to use many parts of himself in the service of the whole self. If a toy is taken away from him, he can reach for it or move toward it and regain possession. If the toy is of great value, removed frequently, or removed in anger, the child may lose the ability to manage with only a part of himself. He lunges at any toy. He starts to howl. His response is total, if less organized and probably less effective than if the part were used.

Real selfness, considered as an organizing principle, operates in an organism, not a machine. It operates with part functions, that may not yet be entirely in the service of the child, in the process of making a whole response. While his resources are slender, his experience slight, and his central core of self not yet solidified, the child may err, overshoot his mark, be retarded in his movement; in short, be temporarily disorganized.

EVALUATING THE WHOLE CHILD

One usually thinks of a child growing toward some goal and becoming in maturity a young man or lady. Without question, the history of each person moves chronologically toward and through phases we call infancy, childhood, adolescence and adulthood. If we examine this notion, we find all too often that adult or artificial norms are applied to the child. An example of this may be seen in families having more than one child. A seven-year old with a younger sibling is given responsibility not commensurate with his age but with his position as "the eldest." The opposite of this is to assume that "he is a child, so one mustn't expect too much."

A somewhat different and more fitting formulation for the evaluation of children's behavior follows: the child must be observed in terms of the extent to which he is able to use the possibilities he has available to him at a given age for the purpose of realizing himself. A three-month-old infant who whimpers, or merely moves restlessly in response to hunger needs instead of yelling lustily, suggests some lowered vitality. A more complex illustration is that of a child of nineteen months who, playing in the park, found a tricycle not in use and proceeded to mount it. Later, the owner, aged four, claimed it. To the nineteen-month-old child, this was an intrusion on his freedom. There were mild to moderate remonstrances from each child and then the four-year old grabbed the other by the neck from behind to pull him from the cycle. The younger one then brought his teeth into action and won the battle. In this situation there were several courses of action open to the younger child. He might have made a healthy tactical retreat, thrown a tantrum, or run to his mother. What he did decide to do was to use an available resource—his teeth—to gain his end. Under the conditions, this was quite rational and natural behavior.

An evaluation of either of the two children cannot be based on this one situation. It is essential that the wholeness of the child be considered. If the nineteen-month-old child resorts to biting in other, less stirring circumstances; if while enjoying free use of hands and legs, he makes his first approach with his teeth, or if he is constantly getting into scrapes with his contemporaries, his performance is then open to other interpretations. We must broaden our evaluation to include much other behavior. Does he bite more or less frequently? Does he have eating difficulties? Does he rebel against all limitations? Is there a quality of compulsive, consuming aggressiveness in him, or a quality of alertness and curiosity? In a word, the child's wholeness—in time and circumstance—must be a part of any evaluation.

Suppose the situation were reversed: the four-year old bites the nineteen-month old. We would have to make the same survey to ascertain the elder child's personality. But we would tend to consider the performance pathological. We would feel it to be abnormal since at four a child has many other possibilities for achieving a constructive solution. He can make an appeal to the judgment of others. He can bide his time, or he can use his strength more constructively to gain his ends. It is not possible to say when one mode of action is within normal limits and when it becomes pathology. It is only possible to make an approximation by taking the above broad view.

NEEDING AND WANTING

During the early months of an infant's life, the most appropriate formulation of his motivation seems to be in terms of "needs" for satisfaction of a physical or physiological nature. Later a different formulation is appropriate. Needs become synthesized with wanting. And wanting implies that choice is entering as a quality of the child. At first one can speak of the choices as the child is observed moving toward one toy or another, or responding differently to different people. Then it seems appropriate to speak of "I want" and "I need." The formulation is still a simple one, and the moves of the child are still fairly simple to conceptualize.

During this time there is an enrichment of experience, a development of inner resources, an exploring and testing of the outside. Each new experience engenders another vista. The child is constantly asking questions with his eyes, his hands, his total movement. As each new physical component develops, as grasping, crawling, standing and walking become available to him, new avenues are opening. All of this requires freedom to choose and to explore.

According to Gesell,[5] two and a half is the age when the spanking curve goes up. By this he indicates an important fact: the child, given a reasonably fortuitous beginning, often starts at this point to assert himself. The stand he takes may frequently be at odds with that of his parents. There is also an increase in safety-seeking, in compulsive drives, and anxiety.

This condition in the child appears to be a more open expression of something whose beginnings may be seen about a year earlier. At eighteen months, or shortly there-after, children who have shown no signs of disturbance very frequently develop sleeping difficulties. The onset varies widely but seems to occur earlier in children whose freedom has been respected than in those who have been routinized. Such a child begins to have difficulty in getting to sleep, or after many months of sleeping uninterruptedly, he may waken during the night. He may waken with a cry, act bewildered and confused. The awakening may be followed by calling for a parent, or, by clambering out of his crib and going to his parents' bed. Usually he is readily soothed and relieved by the closeness of the parent. Often he requires words, a look at the stars or some other familiar object. This may seem to be distracting the child, but in combination they represent something solid, secure, fa-miliar.

This condition is not night terror—*pavor nocturnus*—which is qualitatively different and certainly a more in-tense demonstration of anxiety. There the child is literally paralyzed. He sits in his crib, fists clenched, eyes staring, screaming with all his might. Unlike the first child, his anxiety is not directed toward the constructive end of call-ing for a parent, or of leaving his bed and moving toward more familiar ground.

Regularly in the histories of children between the ages of seven and ten one finds the comment: "He was all right until the age of two-and-a-half. He walked and talked at the proper time and then we began to have trouble." It is important to recall that this is the age when, in Freudian theory, the Oedipus situation becomes paramount in the child's development. Whatever the theoretical formula-tion, there are clinical facts to support the contention that something of a disturbing nature does occur at this age.

The condition in which the child tends to show marked unrest, apparently deficient integration, and a tendency toward what can be called "natural anxiety" can be interpreted as follows. Development in this period is based on infancy. If that has been a crushing experience, it is likely that the unrest of the phase beginning at about eighteen months will be different, and possibly much milder. Further, it seems that the more optimal the earlier months, the sooner will the restless period begin, for essentially it is a very alive searching for a firm foundation, requiring all available energy. It is exceedingly important that this period be understood and dealt with, because less than optimal handling is reflected morbidly in the child's subsequent joy and vitality.

During this time, the child's physiological changes continue, but an entirely new capacity develops that adds another dimension to the individual's personality. I refer here to the development of language, employment of symbols for communication, manipulation and thinking—use of the mind. As with each new possibility, new vistas are opened, new experiences are available, and new dangers are encountered. The elements of time, retentiveness and ideal formation become part of the child's armamentarium. This new modality takes him into the world to a far greater extent, and increases the richness and depth of his real self.[6] Such a transition is not a simple one, not one made smoothly.

This period has its prototype in the Biblical story of Genesis. Eve, tempted by the serpent, utilized the human interest in freedom and curiosity and exploration to further experience. The early innocence and dependence was lost, but knowledge and the chance to make a life for one's self out of one's creative possibilities was gained.

We can view the implications of this addition to the child's resources interpersonally and intrapsychically. In the latter sense, he begins, by symbolizing, to develop concepts. He starts to deal with things in terms of their essence. A child of six to eighteen months will use a book, variously as a missile, a train, a table, or to chew on. Later the book's essential purpose is realized. The pictures are for looking at or for Mommy to explain. Beyond that it becomes something for the child himself to pore over and to "read."

This development is also seen if one follows serially, over several years, the painting of a child. One notes first a messing around with the paint. Brush, hands and arms are used. No limit to the paper is recognized. In time the limits become apparent but color expression dominates. Gradually forms enter which the child seems not to have conceived of at the outset. He may suddenly find a flower, a house or a sun, and his ecstatic remark indicates a revelation rather than an accomplished goal. There is, in a sense, the expression of inner activity, body movement, rhythm and feeling. Between four and five years, he may begin more planning. There is less activity and more concern for form—an indication that the child has a conception that he is trying to realize. In times of stress, he may return in part to the earlier type of work, with emphasis less on form, or "realistic" representation, and more on the feeling qualities. This, incidentally, marks a change from the more complete idea/feeling, concept/percept approach, to a less integrated, or partial notion.

Dreaming seems to develop at this period also. Behavior while awake shows many indications of problem-posing and solving. Alternatives are considered. Normal conflict seems evident. Clinically, during sleep, there is usually an increase in body movement, a likely indication of intra-psychic activity. Such activity in this period could result in anxiety which the child is as yet incapable of facing, or solving in the dream. His awakening is then a consequence. But on awakening with the felt anxiety, another factor enters. This child has entered sleep reluctantly, holding on to the necessary anchorage of his relationship with the known and familiar. The child who is put to sleep by the mother or the nurse wakes calling for her. It is as though he has taken leave of safety, and under the stress of anxiety, reaches back for that point. Not finding it, increased anxiety ensues.

A young child, during waking hours, is able to speak and act in terms of "This is mine. That is not mine." He wants his spoon and knows which belongs to his brother. He errs sometimes, but he rights himself. Then he wakens to a dark room, without bearings, possibly filled with dream symbols. Awakened thus, he is without an anchorage, and he has not yet an adequate base in himself. His pristine state of simple biological reactivity has had another dimension added, giving him greater opportunity for integrating with his world. But it is a double-edged weapon. It adds to his inner activity, and it gives him a daytime frame of reference that is markedly different from his nighttime framework. Earlier, he has wakened to hunger disturbances. These diminish and he sleeps through the night. Then his psychic inner life begins to stir. The first period brought the hunger cry. The second brings the need for feeling safe in familiar territory.

Another consequence of this developing mind is the conceptualizing and the symbolizing of the self. Here it is not selfness in the sense of a dynamic, organizing principle, but a more or less concrete, objectified notion of the self. Watch a two-year-old who has been permitted the experience of answering the telephone rush to it when it rings. Pell mell he goes, shouting, "I do it!" In his eyes there is an expectant gleam, as though he is seeing the whole action before him as an image and is hurrying to make reality catch up with it. Or watch him as he pulls his chair around to "Daddy's place" at the dinner table, or stamps around in outsized house slippers. He is overshooting his mark, but he is trying things out, in terms of a notion about himself.

THE ABILITY TO ABSTRACT

There is another consequence of the child's thinking—his dawning ability to abstract, to universalize out of the particulars around him. He, like the rest of us, lives in a world of particulars. But, unlike an older person, his generalizing is not solid and his particularizing is not fully integrated with his wholeness. The healthy adult is able to know that patience is a virtue, but that impatience is not necessarily an evil. The child cannot do this readily. This is the time when the inconsistency and hypocrisy of parents is especially disturbing. The child who is trying to draw general conclusions finds himself experiencing vagaries which would baffle a more experienced observer.

The most important generalizations the child makes concern himself. Acting on these terms, he is bound to sustain a number of bumps. In his mind he sets up purposes and tries to realize them. For the healthy child these have the quality of constructive goals and ideals. When they are unattainable, failure is not devastating. Interpersonally, however, there may be turbulence when the child uses a word to communicate a wish to his parents and is not understood. After a few attempts to make himself clear, he may say, constructively, "Johnny show you," and run to fetch, or point out the object himself. But, confronted by an unheeding parent, the expressed wish may become a demand, heated by frustration of the new skill.

INDIVIDUAL AND GROUP ACTIVITY

Another aspect of development is seen in play. Gesell [5] has spoken of the movement from parallel play to social or group play. The first relationship is to things such as toys. Two children, or a child and an adult, can be in the same room, each with his own activity. Often, the first togetherness comes in an interest in another person which soon leads to one or the other taking over until the parallel play has turned into lone play. A little later the togetherness has a more cooperative quality.

One boy of three and a half began to play with blocks and made great throughways all around the play room. I was there but not invited to participate. If I entered in any way, I was not ousted, but I was ignored. Later, he began to see a use for me—as a hauler of blocks. The next phase involved his suggestion that I also build a track parallel to his. Of course, here, I had to use the leavings, and often ended up with none. Presently, this was rectified and a different quality developed. He began to build roadways across our two tracks, a tunnel under them, and finally "switching points" where we could exchange cars. For a time, I gradually lost all my cars, or was left with the caboose. Eventually this too changed, and he suggested we work together on a single set of tracks. Each of us had his role and we shared the cars.

Briefly, in the organizing process, the child had progressed from a unit, to a more active social being, to a more complex organization.

While the healthy child creates a self image, the less healthy child begins to develop an idealized image—what Horney [6] calls a comprehensive attempt at solution of conflict. Between the ages of three and five, it is not likely that one will see the fruition of such an attempt at solution, but significant beginnings may be observed and the tools with which to create a solution are present. The categories of moving toward, away from, and against, still suffice. But increasingly, the more complex structures of self-effacement, expansiveness and resignation become applicable. It is also with the development of an idealized image that constructive influences from without are blocked.

A child of four and a half illustrated the self image and the idealized image in evolving this thesis concerning God. She said, "There is a God who is in Heaven. He's good. But I have a God in me, too. He's my guardian. He's here." She pointed to her heart. "But sometimes God makes me bad. Not the one in Heaven, but the one here." She pointed to her stomach.

This seems to be the expression of an externalized idealized image—God "up there"—and an awareness of self, and, to some extent, of an inner-owned idealized image. One comment on the stomach location of the bad God: this little girl has on occasion eaten compulsively. Sometimes she has referred to her "100 stomachs." What better expression of inner emptiness and the voracious appetite of an idealized image?

A CHILD IN TREATMENT

When Joan first came into therapy she was little more than four. My first direct contact with her indicates much about her character at that time. I had seen her mother and had learned something of the child's history. Now the bell rang, and the door opened as I started toward it. Joan's mother seemed to fill the foyer, and I knew—and felt—that there was someone with her. In the next moment I saw a little girl. She was appended to her mother neither like a leech nor an adornment. There was neither dependency nor any indication of a vital attachment. The feeling was strong that the mother, en route, had had a dry leaf blown against her and that in some mechanical way it had clung. Joan was apathetic. Her aliveness could only be hoped for. At my invitation, she accompanied me to the play room. She did not glance backward, she showed no eagerness to come with me, or to stay with her mother. It was as though some force exterior to her merely blew her hither and yon.

Joan was the first born child. Her first two years were considered normal by the parents. After two she was free of wetting and soiling. She was a lively little girl who sang nursery rhymes and performed on request for the guests of the family. There were no gross difficulties in eating, sleeping, walking or talking. She seemed to be of average intelligence and differed little from the usual child at this time.

Then two signal, external events occurred. Joan's mother, who had been in business, became pregnant. Joan was taken over from the nurse by the mother. She then became markedly retarded in all areas. A lively child, she became withdrawn. She played poorly with other children, and a nursery group she was placed with during her third and fourth years found her always on the periphery. Her songs disappeared; in fact, all music seemed to depart from her life. She stopped talking, using only sounds and a kind of gibberish. Toilet habits changed. She occasionally wet and soiled, then retained both urine and stool. She evinced no curiosity, no searching, not even an indication of a fantasy life. Psychometrics administered when she was four showed subnormal scores. In many ways she seemed like one of the cases described by Spitz,[2] although here the onset was in the third year rather than the first.

The following is an evaluation of the situation at the beginning of treatment. Joan had been able to build a backlog of experience in her first two years that gave her some feeling of wholeness. This was on a rather tenuous basis. She had begun to develop some verbalizing resources, but these were largely commandeered and exploited by adults in the service of exhibiting her talent, not herself. In addition, she could never use this resource for herself for requests or demands. Reaching out in other directions for a place for herself had been denied her whenever an error was made. Attempts to use a fork or a spoon were severely criticized when a mess ensued.

Much of this came just at the period that I have suggested is crucial in the child's development: the time when many more excursions are made into social living, and when inner unrest is developing along with this new modality—thinking and symbolizing. Joan responded with withdrawal, a marked loss of interest in growing. It is interesting to note there was not a complete return to earlier toilet habits. In the light of subsequent investigation, this seems to have been her major act of defiance, her way of holding back any expression of herself for her parents. Although not strong enough to lash out in a typical behavior disorder, she hadn't given up her fight completely.

RESPONSE TO TREATMENT

At the start of therapy this child was suspended between a life of interpersonal relations and a life of fantasy. She could not withdraw into fantasy and imagination because just as this resource was opening to her her growth was blocked; and what she had available to use tightened up. It enabled her to shut out much of the world and thus she had little of the outside experience so necessary to childish imagining. A child is not a butterfly whose growth and change while secluded within the cocoon is natural. For children, forced withdrawal from life is an unnatural phenomenon. An older child, forced to withdraw, will at least take his imagination into the shell with him, and whatever little seeps in from the outside will encourage a flourishing, if cancerous, growth of fantasy. Joan, however, did not have even this.

Our sessions began to provide her with the opportunity to experience more. She started out in the middle of the room. Slowly, awkwardly, almost in a sleeping state, she moved from one toy to another. She did not speak to me, nor did she look at me. Reaching out gingerly, she picked up one thing, then another. She squeezed them, smelled them, returned them to their places. She stumbled over blocks or toys scattered on the floor as though they were not there. At the easel she stopped and stood very still for some moments. It was not until several weeks later that she approached the brush rack that was out of her reach, with an obvious desire to paint. She never looked to me for help. When I brought the brushes down, she started to paint. Even in this, there was only a savoring of the most elementary qualities of the paint. Brushes were used as mops. The paint was thrust onto the paper. There was no form, only a riot of color, without rhythm or harmony. After several months this changed. The brushes were stroked, and the colors began to assume a semblance of harmony. Suddenly, the apparently random painting took form, and Joan, with all the nascent energy she could muster, breathed softly, "A tree." And, indeed, one could discern a tree.

Meanwhile a similar movement had been developing with other materials—blocks, clay, a needle and thread. To illustrate one that shows the beginning of increased vocal communication: in the cupboard Joan found the musical toys. She took out the cymbals and began to clang them together with a total lack of rhythm, order, or form. I reached in and took out a set of bells and tried to match her movements, without success. She scarcely noticed me. Two or three weeks later she did the same thing, and this time, since it was possible to detect a pattern, I matched the rhythm a little better. The next session she took both bells and cymbals, began to play by herself, and then handed me the bells. We had our first concert. A few weeks later, Joan spotted animals in the farm scenes on the curtains, and I heard her singing snatches of "Old MacDonald." It was a solo performance meant largely for herself, but soon she sang with awareness that someone was listening. Finally, we sang duets.

Joan's gibberish now became tumbling words. She made some hasty announcements about her brother, then more measured comments about things more related to herself and what she was doing. Today there is still no real back-and-forth, verbal communication, but there is a real beginning. There is also increased alertness—an interest in things outside her home, in the playroom, and in her relation to me.

An essential spark of life, dormant at the beginning of treatment is now far more than a mere glow. The future course will undoubtedly be stormy, but she now has opening vistas for development, awakening interest in seeking a way, and the freedom to expand her resources. She has the possibility of setting up a self image; yes even for setting up an idealized image. But, in either case, there will be richness to work with and a real chance for health.

AN AGGRESSIVE REACTION

Another girl, four and a half, went through her first two years with no evident difficulty. Eating and sleeping, toileting and physical agility were natural. In the third year came the usual sleep disturbances, unrest and anxiety, manifested by crying and fussing at bedtime and during the night. This was met with poor understanding by the parents. The child was threatened; pressure, including spanking, yelling and withdrawal of affection, was applied. The disturbance lasted over a prolonged period, and at four and a half, the child still has anxiety about going to sleep. Following the original disturbance there was a marked decline in courage, interest in people and curiosity. There was temporary return to wetting, always in a defiant, aggressive way not associated with the usual enuresis, i.e. wetting at night.

This was a child with a good start, who, when she ran into difficulties, struck back. There was some withdrawal, but more apparent was compulsive aggressiveness. She had a good backlog of health and spirit, together with more freedom than Joan had, and thus was able to put up a scrap and utilize her imagination and creativity. Evidence of this was in her graphic art. At two and a half she sewed a pattern with needle, colored thread, buttons and buckram. The effect was achieved without plan or obvious intent. Yet, suddenly she exclaimed, "Why, it's a Mexican man!" The resemblance was remarkable. Some time later she painted in the play room, using the brush well, and produced a pleasing color pattern, having rhythm, depth and organization.

The pressure to conform to adult standards continued, however, with some abatement but with sufficient force to facilitate a change of basic movement to one of compliance. Her painting became less spontaneous, less colorful, and very tentative. The pressure was reflected in the diminished joy she had in the work. When I remarked about the difference in her painting from her earlier spontaneity to the current more stilted work she made a most significant remark. "I have to have a nice dream before I can do a nice painting." She still has considerable spark and regularly this bursts through her compliance and shallowness into a flame of rebellion. There is sleep restlessness, often with awakening to report a "bad dream." She told me, "When I'm good, I have bad dreams. And when I'm bad, I have good ones."

One change which seems a consequence of her active struggle for growth and the addition of more constructiveness in relation to herself is a renewed interest in dancing. The agility that was present earlier showed itself in considerable grace in dancing. When the tide turned against her, she responded with a loss of this grace, and occasional attempts to dance were awkward. Recently the return of both interest and rhythm to her whole outlook was reflected in a spontaneous remark, "I forgot how to dance and now I learned again, better."

This little girl already has a far richer personality than Joan. And the richness is reflected in her idealized and self images as a bride, as Dale Evans, Roy Roger's girl friend, a sweet mother, a princess. And in both the above cases there is far more health and hope than in those cited by Dr. Spitz, where aliveness was crushed in the early months and healthy experiencing was nipped in the bud. In such cases, there is almost no possibility to develop even an interesting neurotic character, because the child's resources can hardly lift their heads.

CONCLUSIONS

To conclude with some remarks that apply to all people, but that have greater relevance for children—and paradoxically are least used in that connection: human beings always have the possibility of growing. Growing carries the connotation of purpose and goal-seeking. And, while perfection is included in the goal, the experience and joy of the process are an essential part. Both ideas are necessary for a whole view of growing. It is only when we include the part that says the process itself is a value that we can do fruitful analytic work. Only then can we make cogent observations of behavior. Only then can the important be separated from the unimportant.

So frequently children give the essence of things in simple, striking words. A little boy speaking to Dr. Rasey [7] said, "You know, a pansy bed that's going to be is almost as pretty as a pansy bed that is."

A necessary component of growing is error, by the standard of perfection. The consequence is that movement often fluctuates and takes time in the course of realizing its direction. Again, a child's words tell it. In a cab en route to the office, a little girl saw her parents agitated that the driver might take the wrong street. Calmly, she said, "Let him go his way. If he goes wrong, he can always turn around."

The growing child is engaged in a process. He is vigorously exploiting talents, interests and interpersonal relations. He is faced by a wide variety of outside experiences, and is assailed and supported from within by an increasing reservoir of impulses and capacities. This is the stuff of life, the ambiguous stuff that enters into and moves us all from birth to death, and that each of us embodies in his living.

REFERENCES

1. MacMurray, J., *Reason and Emotion*, Faber and Faber, London, 1935.
2. Spitz, R. A., In *The Psychoanalytic Study of the Child*, I, Anna Freud ed., International Universities Press, New York, 1945.
3. Ribble, M. A., *The Rights of Infants*, Columbia University Press, New York, 1943.
4. Rasey, M., personal communication.
5. Gesell, A., *Infant and Child in the Culture of Today*, Harper & Brothers, 1943.

6. Horney, K., *Neurosis and Human Growth*, W. W. Norton & Co., New York, 1950.
7. Rasey, M., In *Issues in Integration*, The Foundation for Integrative Education, New York, 1948.

A Unitary Theory of Anxiety

HAROLD KELMAN

This is an attempt to begin formulating a unitary
theory of anxiety and to present some of its essentials.
My interest in this subject has many sources. Daily we experience anxiety in ourselves and in the troubled people
we are helping. Both we and they are aware of anxiety in
many aspects of our lives, in the lives of others and in the
world around us. Our time has been referred to as the
"Age of Anxiety."

My interest in dreams, broadened to the dreaming process, and to process in general in theory and in therapy,
has also stimulated my investigation of anxiety. A study
of dreams soon confronts us with anxiety dreams. Many
theories of human nature, motivation, or personality have
had their limitations brought to light in attempting to
understand anxiety dreams.

Methodology and theory building has been a third
source of stimulation for this presentation. Only with
theory can our observations be ordered and brought into

Revision of a paper read in part before the Association for the Advancement of Psychoanalysis at the New York Academy of Medicine
on January 23, 1957. Published in *The American Journal of Psychoanalysis*, XVII, 2, 1957.

meaningful relationship. With a theory we can utilize more productively data already available, data which does not seem to fit well or at all in previous theories, and bring to light new facts.

THEORIES OF ANXIETY

As there have been many theories of human nature or human personality, so have there been many theories of anxiety. It could not be otherwise. As a theory of motivation begins to evolve and expand, it must at some point present its views on anxiety, that ever-present human experience and manifestation of being human. Some have not only dealt with anxiety in their theoretical formulations, but kept revising them. Freud made at least three major revisions of his ideas on anxiety. And we know there was quite some criticism of his ideas on anxiety dreams as they related to his dream theory of wish fulfillment. The content and spirit of his answers to these questionings seemed inadequate and defensive to many. These doubts, plus his own restless searchings, contributed to the revision of his ideas on anxiety again and again.

Just as Freud's theories regarding anxiety evolved and changed, so has there been change in the life history of other theories of anxiety ever since they began to be formulated. The theories led to evaluation and testing, and from these came a sequence of shifts in some essential views regarding anxiety.

In earlier theories of anxiety the assumption was implicit that anxiety is bad, less anxiety better, and no anxiety good. You will recognize in this attitude Freud's pleasure-pain principle and the philosophy of hedonism, promulgated by Bentham, John Stuart Mill, and Jevons. Its essence is that it is in the nature of man to desire pleasure and to avoid pain. So, anxiety which is painful is bad and contrary to man's nature; and no anxiety, which is pleasure and congruent with man's nature, is good. According to this philosophy, the goal of therapy is clearly indicated: to lessen anxiety to the point of zero.

Although many people's lives are governed by hedonistic ethics, more and more men and women are asserting that for our present world such an ethic is neither tenable, human, nor humane. There has been likewise a shift in theories of anxiety. More and more we read that being anxious is an aspect of being human. Existential philosophy and psychoanalysis have contributed significantly to this viewpoint. Anxiety is seen as both paralyzing and stimulating, self-creating and creating the world of which we are a part. Also, anxiety is more often differentiated into sick or irrational anxiety and healthy or rational anxiety. From such an orientation the objectives of therapy are necessarily as follows: to lessen sick anxiety and to increase healthy anxiety.

So that this last statement will not be misunderstood, I wish to amplify it. It means to lessen sick anxiety which causes sick, wasteful and unnecessary suffering, to lessen anxiety that obstructs and distorts healthy growth. Its end is to favor conditions and possibilities for this healthy growth, of which healthy anxiety is a concomitant. It does not mean that the objectives of therapy are to replace the sick anxiety by healthy anxiety, and to leave the total amount of anxiety the same or more than obtained before. As I will point out later, the total amount of anxiety tends to become less as we become healthier, and attitudes toward anxiety, its sources, and its functions change.

Another shift in theories of anxiety has occurred. Anxiety and fear as two distinct and different feelings have become more clearly distinguished. To this delineation Goldstein has made most significant contributions. "In the state of fear, we have an object in front of us which we can 'meet,' which we can attempt to remove, or from which we can flee. We are conscious of ourselves as well as of the object, we can deliberate how we shall behave toward it, and we can look at the cause of the fear which actually lies spatially before us. On the other hand, anxiety *attacks us from the rear,* so to speak. The only thing we can do is to attempt to flee from it without knowing where to go, because we experience it as coming from no particular place. This flight is sometimes successful, though merely by chance, and usually fails; anxiety remains with us. Fear differs from anxiety by its character of defense reaction and by its pattern of bodily expression." [1] This is but a brief quote from Goldstein's extensive and detailed description of these two feelings.

This clear delineation of fear and anxiety represents an important forward step in our understanding of both. Many previous and present theories of fear and anxiety have included both under fear or anxiety, and hence have confused both. This has been particularly true with regard to fear and anxiety dreams in which I have had a special interest. In fact, the recognition of fear dreams as separate and distinct from anxiety dreams has been very little evident in the literature. Clinically, the sick fears, such as phobias, have been identified and described by psychiatrists for a number of years. These fears or phobias are gross categorizations. They are of things, whether the thing is a person, animal, place, or natural phenomenon like lightning. But internal processes are also objectified into things. So we have fears of thoughts, feelings, dreams, and of behavior patterns, such as impulsively uttering in public foul or blasphemous language, or because of stage fright, suddenly losing one's voice or wetting oneself.

The above categorization of fears is essentially a descriptive one. To a dynamic understanding of fears, Horney made a significant contribution.[2] She saw the emergence of these sick fears as a consequence of unresolved conflicts. They emerged when the neurotic structure, evolved to protect against the breaking through of unresolved conflicts, was threatened. The creation of such a structure is to give the individual a feeling—albeit a pseudo feeling— of unity and identity. That fears such as Horney identified would emerge becomes understandable. The fears she wrote about were the fears that the equilibrium of this rigid structure would be disturbed. One expression of this fear of losing one's equilibrium is the fear of insanity. She also mentioned the fear of exposure, and the associated fears of disregard, humiliation, and ridicule. A final fear she discussed at length was the fear of changing anything in oneself. Here we see the fear of anything new, different, unfamiliar, or unknown—in short, of any change in the status quo for fear that what might be could only be worse.

KINDS OF ANXIETY THEORIES

In addition to a differentiation between fear and anxiety, and of the sick and healthy forms, other shifts in theorizing about both have occurred. In keeping with the evolution of medicine and psychiatry, early theories tended to be organic and later ones psychological. Following attempts to explain anxiety on physiological and, later, neurophysiological lines, and in purely psychological and psychoanalytic concepts, psycho-physical theories were attempted. Some were couched in terms of psycho-physical parallelism, and others were suggestive of psycho-physical interactionism. In both, psyche and soma were dealt with as if they were entities. In the first kind of theory, it was as if what happened in soma and psyche went along on parallel tracks. In the second, psyche and soma were again viewed as if separate and interacting on one another.

Gestalt thinking brought with it a new perspective, most clearly evident in Goldstein's holistic viewpoint. The organism is seen as a whole. Psychological and physical are regarded as aspects of that whole. The organism, not as a separate entity but as a performing organism in an environment, becomes the focus of study. The values and limitations of the atomistic and synthetic methods are recognized and the study of wholes is regarded as the more adequate method for studying living organisms in environment.

MEANING OF "NEUTRAL" CONCEPTS

My efforts have been to move this trend several steps further. I operate with the concept that organism-environment is a single, integral reality and that neither can be studied as separated or separable; that the concepts to be used also are applicable to the physical and psychological aspects of both organism and environment. In this sense, the concepts are psychophysically neutral.

This neutrality also implies carrying maximum value judgment as to fact, and minimum value judgment as to morals and aesthetics. As human beings, we are guided by aesthetic and moral values and values as to fact. We make these valuations on what goes on inside and outside ourselves concomitantly. We do it spontaneously and automatically, depending on how healthy or how sick we are. Formulating concepts in neutral terms may act as a corrective to the automatic, compulsive judging—not evaluating —that goes on in us. The more compulsively driven we are, the more we judge in absolutes of good/bad, beautiful/ugly. To what in fact obtains we are too little open, and what little does come through is prejudged and labeled. The more and the longer we can be open to what is inside and outside ourselves, the more we can "see" and "experience" "what is"; the more whole our picture, the more adequate is our basis for making aesthetic and moral valuations of what is. Thus my concepts are guided by the philosophy of *what is* and not by the philosophy of *what ought to be*.

What ought to be deals with imagination, unreality, and irrationality. Horney has dealt extensively with the sickness of "The Tyranny of the Should" [3]—a sick, contradictory system of shoulds, oughts, musts and must-nots that come into being through environmental mediation, are taken over by the individual, and then unconsciously drive him toward human impossibilities, toward actualizing his "idealized image." [4] These "shoulds" coerce him and squeeze down on his human spontaneity. To the extent that a human being is sick he will be governed by contradictory absolutes of what he should be, morally and aesthetically, and his evaluation of fact will be blurred and distorted. To the extent that he is healthy he will be guided by a congruence of his evaluations of facts, morals, and aesthetics—in short, more by the philosophy of *what is* and less by the philosophy of *what ought to be.*

ANXIETY—HEALTHIER AND SICKER

For these shifts in theory to have occurred, it was essential that our theories and therapies more frequently make possible healthy fear and healthy anxiety. Before one is healthier there is a tendency to confuse fear with anxiety and vice versa; also to call by other names a variety of feelings which are expressions of fear and anxiety, and to identify as fear or anxiety a host of other feelings.

Spontaneous verbalizations of patients indicate how they experienced differently what, for the present, I will call healthy and sick anxiety. These are mainly the patients' subjective experiences, with occasional objective observations of themselves in the course of a session. I shall first cite an example from an actual session and then give a composite picture from the associations of a number of patients.

One man had been in a state of massive anxiety from earliest childhood. There was hardly a neurotic pattern that he did not use to deaden or avoid anxiety. As he became older he used sex, food, alcohol, and sedatives to numb it. He was in restless, almost constant flight, manifested by fast walking, fast talking, fast car driving. His thoughts were constantly racing. All the "general measures to relieve tension" that Horney [5] described were manifest to an extreme degree. As might be expected, nightmares were common. In addition, to avoid anxiety he lived a most constricted and restricted life. It is amazing that with all this suffering and constricted existence, he got a college and law-school degree, and did fairly well in a subordinate position in a large law firm. The tragedy was that he worked and lived far below his potential.

In the course of our work which, understandably, proceeded very slowly, even the slightest move closer to himself precipitated intense anxiety followed by flight. As we proceeded he told me he had had recurrent diarrhea almost all his life, always perspired profusely, panted, had easy and extreme tachycardia; and I observed, even in winter, moisture on his upper lip and forehead and a flushed face. He usually went without a coat, even in very cold weather. On occasion, not too infrequently, he would feel cold and shiver even on a hot day. His hands were rarely dry; mostly they were cold and moist, as were his feet.

His patterns for numbing and avoiding anxiety slowly became resolved. The somatic manifestations of anxiety slowly diminished and his restricted life slowly began to expand. After a number of years of analysis, he said in a session, "I feel anxious but it's different." There was a surprised, pleased tone in his voice. "It's different from the other kind of anxiety I used to feel. I feel warm. I want to stay with it. It feels like it's mine and belongs to me. That other anxiety was cold. It didn't seem to be mine. It was alien. It seemed to come from outside of me. I used to feel overwhelmed by it, helpless, paralyzed and wanted to run away. I'd get desperate."

The following is a composite of a number of patients' verbalizations regarding these two different kinds of anxiety. What I am calling healthy anxiety, they described as "mine." "It starts in me, it belongs to me, it is inside of me. I can stay with it. I want to stay with it. It's alive. I feel warm with it. I feel it gives me a push. It's uncomfortable, but I don't want to run away. My heart doesn't go fast like it used to. My guts don't knot up like they used to when I was anxious. My hands are warm and dry. I don't feel too restless with it."

About the other anxiety they had experienced, which I am calling sick anxiety, they said, "That other anxiety I used to feel and still do. Sometimes it terrified me and I had to run. I'd get desperate and frantic. I'd get terribly restless. My hands would get cold and sweaty. My heart would race. My gut would go in knots. I'd suddenly have to make it to the bathroom. That anxiety was cold. It felt alien. It felt like it came from outside. I felt like it was pushed on me. It descended on me. I felt it as ominous, implacable. I felt helpless. I felt paralyzed. Sometimes I'd go rigid. In the nightmares it was the worst. I'd go rigid and paralyzed and I couldn't utter a sound. My muscles and my voice simply wouldn't function."

Only after these patients, well on their way toward improving, had experienced more aspects of the sick anxiety that had obtained most of the time hitherto and still recurred from time to time but not in its former intensity and extensity, could they begin to experience more and more healthy anxiety and differentiate it from the sick.

ANXIETY—HEALTHIER AND SICKER—IN DREAMS

Just as I have differentiated healthy from sick anxiety as subjectively experienced by patients, now I want to amplify these differences by some dream sequences and examples. They dynamically describe and contrast what obtains in the earlier and later phases of analytic work. They exemplify the earlier predominant identification with neurotic pride, and being compulsively driven by neurotic processes. They differ from the later periods when more of the patient's energies are becoming invested in constructive patterns of living. They also offer an opportunity for conveying something about the dreaming process and about symbolizing, and show that the dreaming process can only be understood in terms of the individual session in which the dream is mentioned in the total context of the analysis to date. They also tell us something about the points at which anxiety appears in the earlier and later phases of analysis.

When one patient began analysis he had severe insomnia and had to drink himself to sleep nightly. Sex, incessant talking, and a variety of forms of physical activity were among the main ways he benumbed himself, avoided and fled from anxiety. He had many of the physical manifestations of anxiety, including urinary urgency and diarrhea. In time, the amount of liquor required to knock himself out diminished and he was getting to sleep at one and two instead of five and six in the morning.

As we progressed in our work, he reported falling off to sleep and almost immediately awakening in a panic, falling off to sleep again after a while to go through the same sequence many times during the night. Eventually, he became aware that he had dreamed, and in time could recall that the dreams contained a threatening figure. Later he could identify the figure as a man; as the sequence evolved it might be a woman, an animal, an object, like an oncoming automobile, or various combinations of these. With the abating of his general level of tension the dreams became more detailed and seemed to last longer. At first he fled in panic immediately and awoke. Later, he remained dreaming before panic awakening supervened. Finally, he might even move toward the figure. Then he began to feel what he called fear, which changed to panic, followed by awakening and by the subjective experience and objective manifestations of intense anxiety. In one dream he was arguing with the threatening figure while going through some rapid thought processes about how to outwit him. Finally he said to himself, "I'll disturb myself if I keep on with this vociferating, and so I will wake myself up."

In one phase of this sequence of dreams, he debated with himself whether he should stay in it or wake himself up. He had learned through many experiences that if he woke himself, turned the light on, smoked a cigarette, and perhaps read a little, he could then go back to sleep and sleep the night through. Sometimes he decided to stay in the dream. As time went on, he could more often ride through the panic that occurred and continue sleeping. At other times the panic reached frantic proportions. When he woke after such a dream, he knew that sleep was impossible for the rest of the night.

Other patients have described similar debates or actual physical struggles in dreams, in which they sometimes awakened themselves; at other times decided to stay with it, successfully riding through the fear and anxiety; and at other times awoke in various intensities of anxiety. In some instances, having awakened, they would become infuriated and make themselves go back to sleep to finish off the dream and make it come out a triumph. Others, while awakening, would change the dream so that it came out with themselves the winner. Of this dream transforming process they became aware only later in analytic work.

In the longer sequence and in the individual instances I have described, the common denominators are of a struggle between the dreamer and another figure, with the process ending in anxiety. The anxiety in and after the dreams, and often while relating them in sessions, had predominantly the attributes of sick anxiety. Naturally, this is my evaluation because they had as yet not experienced healthy anxiety with which to compare the anxiety they were having. As far as they were concerned, there was only one kind of anxiety.

In the above dreams, the dreamer appears as himself and is identified with himself. In the dream and in his associations, he regards the other figure as threatening to him, to what is vital to him, to what has subjective value for him. But he is not aware that what have subjective value for him are neurotic pride positions, a predominantly neurotic and idealized conception of himself in the maintenance of which, and invested in which, are more, if not most, of his energies. He has little connection with what is healthier in himself, and all too little of it is available. In the sequence of dreams just described, what threatened in the symbol of the other figure was simply other, or different, or slightly less neurotic, patterns which at best contained some aspects of varying degrees of constructiveness. These patients felt threatened primarily by movement and change, and in varying degrees by the dynamism in and the momentum of the analytic process moving them in the direction of what could be healthier, though they were still at a distance from it. Notions of what threatens and what is threatened will be more rigorously defined later.

The following is an anxiety dream in the later phases of an analysis, where, at least in the process manifested in dreaming, the patient as himself is predominantly identified with constructive solutions. That the meaning of this dream was not at a distance, but close, was evidenced by feelings and associations in the session in which the patient related the dream, and from what evolved in the analytic process in subsequent sessions. I will first give the dream as he related it, and then fill in further parts that came up in associations and in answer to my questions. More aspects of the feeling tone and content of the dream kept coming up in subsequent weeks. I would ask questions to help him explore associations that pointed to feelings and patterns in the dream and related to it. This is what we refer to as working with a dream and helping a patient experience it meaningfully. This is conducting an analysis on the basis of a deeper awareness of the analytic process.

He related the dream in the first session after a summer vacation in the Colorado mountains. In the dream the place and terrain were identical. He had been talking about increasing wanting-feelings while on vacation, and also of a deeper awareness of his compulsiveness, which frightened him. I asked him for more on these feelings and he said, "Well, I'll tell you a dream. I was on the top of a mountain in Colorado and sliding down the mountain, but also there was a rhythm about it. Then I started thinking and saw a guy slide off into the air. Then I grabbed and feared I'd fall off. I woke up." Asked what he felt when he woke up, he said, "It was feeling the compulsiveness. I was sensing it building up gradually. I was afraid of its getting out of hand wildly." He was referring to his compulsive thinking and the compulsion to think with which he was very familiar and which appeared when he became anxious. His next association was a dream in which he was patting a woman on the behind. Associations—but more often dreams—of being with, holding, touching, kissing, or having sexual relations with a woman were an old and familiar response to being anxious. Deep and extensive morbid dependency on everyone in the world, and particularly on women, had been a long and prominent feature of our analytic work. By the time of the dream, it had lessened considerably in intensity and extensity.

In the session in which he related the dream and in subsequent ones, much more was added to make up this reconstructed, more detailed description of the dream: "I was sliding down a mountain in Colorado. The road was covered with ice. It had many sharp turns with sharp drops along the side. I had a paper under my behind, like kids do when they slide down a sand hill. I was guiding myself around the curves. I noticed as I went along that a rhythmic feeling developed. I noticed I was learning as I went along and was getting better at it. Many other people were doing the same thing. I was involved with what other people were doing. I saw a young fellow in front of me go off into the air as we came to a sharp turn. I was surprised in the dream that it didn't bother me. I kept on going. A little further on I began to think that could happen to me. With that I got frightened, grabbed for the road and woke up frightened, grabbing the bed."

In the dream he is himself; the situation one in which he had actually recently been. What he is identified with indicates not only moves in a constructive direction, but also actual present constructiveness. He is coming down, guiding himself. His behind is next to the ground and he is doing something he did as a child. He is doing the same as others and is involved with others. Also in the process of dreaming there is an awareness and deepening of a feeling of rhythm and learning while going. He then confronts himself with: "This will happen to you if you continue in this constructive direction. You will get killed like the young fellow in front of you." That he said,

"That young guy in front of me went off into space," has its own special meaning. This confrontation is already a threat, an indication that tension is beginning to mount and, in theoretical terms, evidence of passively externalized self-hate. He said, "And then I began to think." Translated into process terms this would mean: as the tension began to rise, and the threat of anxiety became more imminent, he fell back on his neurotic solution of compulsive thinking. But this solution did not stave off the mounting tension and the already experienced fear and anxiety; it even made it worse because he already had become aware in our work of the destructive nature of this compulsive thinking. This he indicated by his very first associations after the dream, when I asked him what he felt as he woke. He said that he feared this compulsive thinking would get wildly out of hand. He said he was frightened when he woke, but what he actually described was a picture of intense fear and moderately severe anxiety.

In this example, in contrast to the series I mentioned above, the man is himself, but predominantly identified with solutions moving him in the direction of greater health. Also they are in fact predominantly constructive. What threatens then is the presence of, and the emergence of, more constructiveness. What is threatened are residual neurotic solutions still felt subjectively as vital to him. In this dream the neurotic solution that was threatened—and at the same time used to avoid the emerging anxiety—is the neurotic solution of the supremacy of the mind. But as I said above, this makes it even worse, because he has by this time become aware of its destructive implications. The fear and anxiety experienced in this instance, in contrast to the first dreams mentioned which were predominantly sick, were more in the direction of health, and factually, in some measure healthy. What occurred in the next months' work affirmed what I have indicated.

This example also paves the way for what I will later develop—namely, that anxiety per se is not sick or healthy, but is so in its proportions. And the proportions of the anxiety that are sick and healthy are determined by the sources of, the functions of, and the attitudes toward the anxiety and fear. Even from what little I have presented of this case, we can see two sources of anxiety—the experience of central conflict and of self-hate—from neurotic positions being threatened. The function of anxiety was to remind him that the situation was getting uncontrollable and might become disastrous. His attitude toward his fear and anxiety was more on the rational side, though I am aware of some of his irrational attitudes toward anxiety. Anxiety is pain and he feels he should not suffer pain; avoiding pain is justifiable. Of this attitude he has become more aware, because he said, "In the past weeks I became aware how I resisted discomfort instead of accepting it and going along with it." And of central conflict, his discomfort with it and residual attempts to avoid it, he was also becoming aware. In these next associations is delineated the conflict between movement in a constructive direction and the pull toward the neurotic solution of the supremacy of the mind: "I feel clogged up. I feel clogged up and stopped up with being and thinking. I feel clogged up with akin feelings and verbalizations."

THE USE OF ANALOGIES

Analogies can help us understand some of the process terms to be used in the formulation of a unitary theory of anxiety. Analogies and metaphors, at one time excluded from scientific thinking, are finding greater acceptance but with clear delineations of their boundaries of value. Analogies help us get a feeling for abstractions, for theoretical constructs. They help point up what we are talking about; they indicate possible directions for new areas of investigation. They are poetic, denotative, and afford a vision of possibilities. Theory is also vision, but it is connotative and prose. It requires that rigorous criteria be fulfilled for confirmation. While analogies point at and to reality, and theory is about reality, neither theory nor analogy, prose nor poetry *are* reality. They are symbols attempting to communicate reality in different ways.

The process terms which I wish to illuminate by analogy are *system, integration, environment, tension.* These are neutrally descriptive words and contrast with the emotively, aesthetically and morally value-toned words I shall be using in my analogy. This does not make morally and aesthetically toned words better or poorer than value-toned words in regard to fact. Each category of words is best for what it attempts to communicate. But because of an intense emotional response on the part of some people to the idea of neutrally descriptive words, I have attempted to find other words to convey my meaning. The words *comprehensive, totalistic, holistic,* and *integral* suggested themselves but I felt they would confuse more than help, because they are so morally and aesthetically value-laden.

Neutrally descriptive terms, it may be hoped, will act as a corrective to our unwitting, unconscious, automatic, and compulsive moral value-judging, or to be more accurate, value-condemning. The latter almost always prevents our being open to what is spontaneously emerging. In analytic practice we soon become aware of how often our patients think and feel in either-or categories, in absolutes, in finalistic terms, in right/wrong, good/bad, black/white, beautiful/ugly, for/against categories. But it may take them years before they become aware of and resolve this compulsive, dualistic, destructive pattern. The more we can be impartially aware of what is emerging from within and being perceived without, the more we can be open to our processes without prejudging, condemning or exalting, the more we can be neutrally aware of and describe —the more spontaneous and whole we will become. Then, having felt and described *what is,* the more accurate, adequate, appropriate and genuinely human will be all the valuations of our experience—factual, moral and aesthetic. These valuations, of course, go on concomitantly. What I am attempting to communicate are ways to help them become more human, more genuine, more rational and much less dictated by compulsive and contradictory moral and aesthetic "shoulds," which choke off spontaneity and block our healthy growth.

The analogy I wish to use is the R.M.S. *Queen Mary* crossing the Atlantic Ocean during peacetime and again in World War II, when it served as a troopship. In both instances, the ocean is in constant motion. The ship is in motion in the water. Many parts inside the ship are moving, as are many of the people aboard it. Although the physical aspects of the ship may seem to be static, they, too, are constantly changing. In other words, here are individuals in an environment of constant flux and change.

First let us make the time June or July, when the ship is loaded with vacationers eagerly anticipating their European holidays. A quick, smooth crossing, clear, shining days, clear, moonlit or starry nights, and a sea as calm as glass is the environment the passengers would find most relevant to their mood. The sources of tension on the boat would come mainly from feelings of joy, anticipation and exuberant spirits, from the activities of the passengers, and from the crew, working at a peak level, fatigued by toil but happy in anticipation of the tips to be received. Passengers and crew might total four thousand persons. Some of the passengers might grumble about over-crowding, or that the sea was too calm or uninteresting, attitudes which would raise the general tension level.

The same ship in wartime carried up to fifteen thousand troops at one time. The over-all internal and external environment was one of turmoil, conflict, and tension. The immediate, ever-present, relevant environment was right over the ship's side from which a submarine or a Nazi sea raider might strike. Crowding on board was extreme; however that was a minimal source of tension. Tension was fed from inside and outside the boat: the atmosphere of war; the constant threat of attack; the fears of the soldiers on board, the crew manning the guns and safety devices, the engine crew; and the engines driving this mammoth ship through the water at better than thirty-one knots, or on a zig-zag course to outwit enemies.

And the weather was another potential enemy. The last thing the *Queen* wanted was clear days and nights and a calm sea, and that is what the enemy most wanted. This clearly illustrates the relativity of environments. In good weather the ship was a much easier target, much more likely to encounter danger and forays with the enemy. As the *Queen* always went unescorted and depended on speed, maneuverability and her own guns and protective devices for defense, slight rain, haze, fog and moderately choppy seas were ideal for her. They didn't slow her speed too much, but they cut down visibility for her enemies and offered many more opportunities to hide. Very heavy weather was not as bad as very clear weather, but it cut her speed so that she might become a target in a chance encounter with the enemy, and might be hit before she could get away. Heavy weather also slowed her in reaching her destination with her cargo of much-needed troops.

Using the analogy of the *Queen Mary* in peacetime and in war, I have attempted to convey a feeling for the hierarchy of systems, and the interrelationship and relativity of organism and environment. I have tried to indicate that environmental relevance is not determined by physical proximity but by total functional value to the organism, and that the same environment may have different meanings to two different participants, as shown by the example of moderately bad weather, which was favorable to the *Queen,* unfavorable to her enemies. I have also indicated something about tension; that tension has physical and psychological sources within and without, and that it may come from intense feelings of happiness and joyful anticipation and from productive work as well as from fear and threats of destruction. Tension per se is neither good nor bad. To evaluate tension, we must know the sources, the functions, the attitudes toward it, its total amount and its qualities. Thus having detailed it with an analogy, using poetic language and metaphors, the prose and the abstract aspects of the unitary theory of anxiety may be more understandable.

UNITARY THEORY OF ANXIETY

The unitary theory of anxiety is an aspect of a unitary theory of organism.[6] It assumes "organism-environment" as a single unitary process having direction, not purpose.[7] Organism is constituted of a hierarchy of systems, governed by a system principle.[8] This principle we call the tendency toward self-realization.[9] The organism is an aspect of the wider system of organism-environment, which is an aspect of the still wider system, nature or cosmos.[10] Environment for the organism is what has immediate relevance for its self-realizing. Many environments exist for the organism at a particular time. Only a limited number of environments are adequate for the organism's self-realizing. For ultimate self-realization, environments of immediate and ultimate relevance must be moving toward congruence.

By self-realizing we mean the innate tendency in all human beings to move toward realizing what is possible for them as individuals and as members of the human race. The tendency toward self-realizing is operating whether the person is becoming healthier or sicker. In order for self-realizing to go on immediately and ultimately, it is essential for the organism to maintain itself as a whole, as a unity and in a state of relative constancy.[11] The latter two tendencies have been referred to as the tendency toward self-preservation. A detour through physical and/or psychic illness in the service of immediate self-preservation may be dictated by inner and outer circumstances, and may afford a later possibility for self-realizing.

SELF-REALIZING DURING AND THROUGH PHYSICAL AND
MENTAL ILLNESS

This can be seen in the case of a silent ruptured peptic ulcer, where the physical manifestations are predominantly in the foreground, and in a psychotic break, where psychological disturbances are most manifest. The initial hemorrhage acutely reminds this man of a physical illness. He is incapacitated, his body is given a chance to rest and to heal. He will receive the necessary immediate physical treatment, and a diet and a regimen for living when he leaves the hospital. He may also be informed that he needs analytic help, receive it, and benefit therefrom. This set-back, this detour, painful and costly, may seem to have been necessary before the man could become aware of physical and psychological sick processes going on in him, and could seek and receive the help that brought him further along the road to self-realizing than he had ever been.

Similarly, a person may have to suffer a psychotic break before he will seek analytic help. In the course of it, while hospitalized or incapacitated at home from following his previous life pattern consciously or unconsciously, an opportunity has been forced upon him for much inner reorientation and long overdue self-examination. Physical conditions requiring treatment that he was unaware of or had neglected may also be discovered for him. Because of the particular structure of their psychological illness, some people have to have a breakdown—in degrees all the way to a psychosis—before they will receive treatment or take a look at themselves. There are those people who literally have to have their backs to the wall, or be knocked down flat on their back—in short, have to be made helpless by life circumstances they have created—before they will seek help for themselves. They have to humiliate and humble themselves, or cause it to be done to them, before they become open and available enough for human help. In such instances—as in the case of the man with the ruptured ulcer—setbacks are suffered. While receiving treatment, both men, still alive, maintaining themselves at different levels of relative constancy, were concomitantly tending toward self-realization, and ultimately would be further along that road than they had ever been before.

INTEGRATING

This is an attempt to understand the system "organism-environment" through concepts which are psychophysically neutral—i.e., concepts equally applicable to the physical and psychological aspects of the system, organism-environment.[12] Methodologically empirical observation, descriptive analysis, theoretical inference and system thinking have been used in aiding the formulation of these concepts. The experimental situation of therapy was used for their validation and invalidation. Basic is the philosophy of *what is* in contrast to a philosophy of *what should be*.

The central concept I operate with is integration.[6] I assume that living is integrating. Integrating is the pattern of living. Our task then is to define the patterns in the process of integrating. Above, I said that the unitary hierarchical system, organism-environment, has direction. Either aspect, organism or environment, may be moving in the direction of greater health or greater illness—i.e., greater rationality or greater irrationality.[13]

Let us look, for example, at a hierarchical system—a marriage. Husband and wife are environment for each other in degrees of relevance from immediate to ultimate. As a whole, either one might be moving toward greater health or greater illness. This is often brought sharply into focus and more clearly seen when one partner seeks or is forced into analysis by the other. As therapy proceeds and the movement toward self-realization becomes clearer, which one is in fact the sicker of the two becomes more evident —who may in fact have been moving toward greater illness, and who is now moving toward greater health becomes unmistakable. The patterns of integrating in both aspects of the hierarchical system—being married as husband and wife—can be more or less rational and irrational. Put in other terms, there are in husband and wife different intensities and extensities of sickness and health. In each organism—husband and wife—there are conflicting and cooperating patterns.

AGREEING AND DIFFERING—RATIONAL AND IRRATIONAL

The same obtains in the environment. Cooperating patterns in both aspects can cooperate and conflicting patterns in both aspects can conflict. The organism is an autonomous unity—i.e., is governed by laws according to its nature. Environment, immediate and ultimate, is governed by its laws, which are different from those of the organism—i.e., are heteronomous.[7] But heteronomous does not mean opposed. A crucial error is frequently made in making "different" and "opposed" synonymous. Difference makes possible unity in diversity, while opposition fosters irreconcilable conflict and narrows the possibility of cooperation. Greater cooperation and less conflict in nature and man become more possible as we understand more fully the nature of each—and that they are two aspects of one unitary process.

For more healthy cooperation and conflict, a deeper

feeling for differing and agreeing must obtain. Difficulties arise when differing and being different are experienced as being opposed, and agreeing and being agreeable are unconsciously, and often not so unconsciously, experienced as submerging oneself or merging to lose one's identity, or being dominated. This point can be brought out more sharply in a familiar everyday concurrence. John says, "I see it differently. Let's talk about it some more." Mary, in tears, retorts, "It was all so different when we first married. Everything I suggested you loved me for. Now you are against everything I say." Another couple: Mother and Sue, age sixteen, are discussing daughter's previous and new dates. Dad retorts, "Daughter like mother. All women are the same. All women stick together. All they are out for is to use a guy and drop him." In both examples we have false overgeneralizations, black-and-white thinking; if you are not for me you're against me, you are my friend or my enemy; and the finalistic, static attitude obtains: it always was and will be forever. In such an atmosphere, there is compulsive argument on a compulsive, hyper-personal basis, and little discussion of issues in the context of individuals, with the possibilities for clarification and enrichment through similarities and differences, through cooperating and conflicting patterns of integrating.

The sociological implications of agreeing and differing are considerable, and very much under discussion at present. The notions that *agreeing* and *being the same as* are good, and *differing* and *being different from* are bad, are rampant today on the American scene. They are having some pretty disastrous consequences for individuals and groups as well as for the whole nation, for genuine individuality and possibilities for healthier communing and relating. At one extreme we are seeing all too much automatic agreement and conformity, and at the other destructive individual and group rebellion and nonconformity. The seriousness of the situation is reflected in the amount of literature devoted to it and the number of movies, plays and TV scripts on these subjects.

TENSION

All processes in nature are active; passivity is an appearance. That which is apparently passive or permanent or static, in contrast to that which is active, impermanent, changing, in process, or dynamic, is only apparently so. They are apparently so because the rate of change in one is so slow it looks permanent, and the rate of change in the other is rapid enough to be observed, and hence is described as in flux. As all processes in nature are active, they also are phasic. I speak of the organism as always integrating, as continually going through the phases of disintegrating and reintegrating, whether the direction of change is toward greater health or greater illness. Integrating and reintegrating, therefore, are neither good nor healthy, and disintegrating neither bad nor unhealthy. They are merely neutrally descriptive terms.

As it is natural for all organismic processes to be active and phasic, so it is natural for the organism always to be in tension. Conflict and cooperation are as essential to living as is tension. Just as dualistic good/bad thinking and categorizing is applied to so many areas of one's living, so it is to the notion of tension. The dictum is that tension is bad. Therefore, more tension is worse, less tension better, and no tension is good. Tension is bad because it means discomfort, pain. And with pain and pleasure, a similar attitude obtains. Pain is bad, pleasure is good. I have discussed this hedonistic philosophy earlier. According to the philosophy of what is and not what ought to be, pain is pain and pleasure is pleasure, and both—like tension—are natural and essential to living. This is not to suggest pain and tension for suffering's sake, but to help resolve sick attempts to fight and deny the fact of both, which patterns increase the pain or the numbing of it, at the expense of our genuine humanity.

Our objective in therapy is to lower the general level of tension and to lessen tension which is sick in quantity and quality. We are out to resolve sick attitudes toward tension, its sick sources and the sick functions it serves. The amount and quality of tension will then be relatively and predominantly healthier. That tension can be the motor, the impetus and the source of energy for productive work, for self-creating and creating in general is too little appreciated. This kind of tension, in optimal intensity, is essential for creative work. Many artists have described it in detail. Freud also wrote about it with reference to himself. He said he was least creative when he was overly depressed or elated. He worked best in a mood of moderate tension, discomfort, and a little on the depressed and irritable side.

Tension has physical and psychological aspects. Patterns of integration are tension-producing and tension-reducing. One man's associations clearly describe these points. He had been telling me about his problems in reading. He would read a while, feel mounting tension, drop the book, smoke a cigarette, get up and walk around, look in the refrigerator, go talk to his wife, call up a friend. In between, he would go back and read a few pages more and then have to leave it again. This he did most of the evening, finally skimming the pages and chapter headings and ultimately saying to himself that he had got the essence of what the author was communicating.

He said, "I started to read last night, and again I had the same feeling I had at the end of yesterday's session. I felt a rising tension. I can't put it into words. It's as though something was coming up inside of me and something was pushing down from outside, and I had to resist it and to throw it off." He then described the sequence of the night before, and the argumentative, unsuccessful dialogues he was having with himself to "stop this nonsense" and continue with his reading. I then asked him to tell me more about his bodily feelings during the process of the night before. "I've said to you on several occasions, 'I'm jumping out of my skin.' That's the feeling. As though there is something containing me and I have to break through. I imagine I know how my wife feels. I've seen it many times. As reality limits her, her guts blow up. I've seen her with a dress on that's very loose and she had to pull it in at the side. In an hour I can see her stomach distended and her dress is as tight as can be. There is pressure all over my body and pressure in on me, constricting me."

He then told me he had a long lunch hour and that he had many things he planned to do. But even thinking about doing them and about whether he would get them all done set off the same sensations of unbearable tension. He had more than ample time to do his errands, but as the feeling of tension mounted a whole day seemed inadequate for them. "It's just too much. I really have a feeling of being constricted by this physical pressure. Right now I feel, I feel something and I go blank. I feel pressure on my chest. I feel something has got to give." He then went on about the many ways he avoids the feeling of increasing tension when something does not give. They included many of what Horney called "general measures to relieve tension." [5]

They are alienation from self, externalization of inner experience, compartmentalization or psychic fragmentation, automatic control, and operating on the belief of the supremacy of the mind. The key word to bear in mind is "relieve." The measures relieve the painful, subjective awareness of tension but at a price. The person becomes sicker and his general level of tension rises, though he may be unaware of it because he has benumbed himself. So these measures to relieve tension are patterns of integration which are tension-producing.

Self-deceiving and self-seducing patterns may function so effectively and destructively that the opposite—benumbing and not the increase in tension—are experienced. Relief at escape from the awareness of increase of tension is exalted to the heights of ecstasy. In a dream one man was literally and figuratively moving along on his own feet, feeling and knowing what he was doing, guiding and directing someone else. From our work together he knew he had fought against being moved into this position, and whenever he momentarily experienced himself being responsible to himself—and worse still responsible for someone else—he experienced in a flash anxiety and unbearable tension and took flight. Suddenly in the dream there was a switch. The smaller figure he had been responsible for a second before became large and powerful and was completely taking care of him. "It's as though I'm doing something I know, but it's almost effortless, as if the direction is coming from the outside and I feel this ecstasy that is so intense that it's unbearable and I pass out but am not unconscious." The rest of the dream manifested processes of increasing alienation. He then talked of his awareness of the process in the dream. He gave many instances of it and then said, "The moment of release is the moment of escape into imagination."

Later in our work, when he again had similar feelings of something coming up from inside and something pushing down from outside, something did give. The discomfort with the tension was not so great. He bore with the pain more. He did not resort to tension-relieving patterns, but in being able to experience and bear with the pain more he was integrating more with patterns which were tension-reducing in the immediate and in the longer run, although at such moments the subjective awareness of tension and the pain were more intense. This example elucidates the importance of neutral concepts, such as tension, and of patterns which are tension-producing and tension-reducing. It shows how subjective awareness of tension alone is not an adequate criterion of the tension level. In this and in many other examples, general measures to relieve tension became less evident as tension-reducing patterns of integration became more evident, but subjective awareness of tension increased, while objective evidences of tension, such as spasm in striated and smooth muscle or vascular hypertension, became less.

TENSION AND ANXIETY

Tension in the system, organism-environment, oscillates above and below a mean. When tension exceeds the mean variation, the organism tends through its patterns of integration to equalize that tension toward that "mean." [14] The consequences of that phase of equalizing might be that the organism becomes sicker or healthier. As the individual becomes sicker, the mean level of tension rises and the mean variation of tension narrows. As the individual becomes healthier, the mean level of tension steadily decreases and the mean variation of tension widens toward an ultimate, humanly possible and commensurate with continued living. Likewise when the upper human limits are exceeded, death ensues.

With each phase of disintegration and reintegration, organismal tension oscillates above and below its mean. When that mean variation is exceeded and equalization toward the mean is not possible, anxiety appears. The presence of anxiety is determined from the viewpoint of the observer. The person observed may be aware subjectively of being anxious and may objectively reveal physical manifestations of anxiety. On the basis of subjective reports or objective findings and certainly on the basis of both, I would say he is being anxious. I feel that subjective awareness as the sole criterion of being anxious, with its overemphasis on the psychological aspect of anxiety, as well as the requirement of subjective and objective evidence, have blocked our understanding of anxiety.

It is in the nature of the organism to become and be anxious, as it is for it to have fear, joy, anger and sadness. Each of these feelings may be more or less rational and irrational. Each has its specific patterns, with both physical and psychological aspects. The patterns of fear and anxiety are distinct and different, physically and psychologically. Failure to see and make this clear distinction has blocked our understanding of fear and anxiety, and of dreams containing them.

It is not good or bad that the organism is becoming and being anxious, because being and becoming anxious are natural to the organism. Anxiety is cued off—i.e., it is the organism's response to the stimulus of tension having exceeded the mean variation. To use Cannon's term: it is an expression of the wisdom of the body that knows that its homeostatic system is no longer adequate to the given environment.[15] As Goldstein would put it, it is evidence of and a reminder that the organism is now in a state of disorder. Anxiety is cued off when tension develops beyond the mean due to the organism's attempts to integrate in an environment for which it is not adequate and which is not adequate for it. Anxiety appears in the phase of disintegration of the natural cycle, disintegrating-reintegrating, as aspects of integrating. When tension beyond this mean variation is generated in the system, organism-environment, the disintegrating phase is moved beyond its mean phasic limits and anxiety becomes manifest. The pattern of disintegrating beyond the mean phasic limits is the pattern of anxiety. As Goldstein would say, the multiple attempts of the organism to become adequate to its environment are the small shocks to existence. They are what he calls "catastrophic reactions." When the disintegrative phase goes beyond the limits of the mean variation in its attempts at integrating in a system where tension beyond the mean is present, the tendency of the organism to maintain itself as a whole, in a state of relative constancy, and to realize itself, are all threatened. The anxiety cued off is an evidence of and a reminder to the organism that the phase of disintegration has gone beyond the mean limits, and patterns of integration must be utilized to set in motion the phase of reintegrating. This is effected by seeking and finding an external environment and/or creating an internal environment to which the organism is adequate and which is adequate for it.

You may have noted that I have spoken of tension being

moved beyond the mean, anxiety being cued off, anxiety appearing, anxiety becoming manifest. This language is not accidental. It is language that neutrally describes and communicates the feeling of it *happens*, or *what is happening*. I do not speak of anxiety being caused by the exceeding of the mean level of tension. I feel that causal thinking —A causes B—possibly a special form of relational thinking, has been inadequate for understanding anxiety. System thinking is essential. A *may* follow B in a sequence, but this is quite different from being caused by B. Both A and B are determined, but not in the sense of strict causal determinism. They are determined in the sense of being based upon, and an outcome of, the whole system, organism-environment—spontaneous and plastic as well as automatic and rigid processes in man and nature.

To repeat, anxiety may be cued off by changes in tension beyond the mean whether the organism is moving toward greater health or greater illness. Anxiety always arises in the organism. Exceeding the mean tension variation in the organism, which cues off anxiety, does not have its sources solely in the environment, but in the unitary process, organism-environment. Organism or environment do not exist in *vacuo* or as isolated systems or entities. The level of tension in the system, organism-environment, determines the level of tension in the organism. Stimuli arising in both, predominantly now in one and now in the other, effect those changes in the level of tension which the organism tends continually to attempt to equalize toward a mean.

A physical analogy may help visualize this notion. Picture a horizontal tube with its ends closed. Opening into it and extending upright are three tubes, open at the top. Label the upright tube at either end of the horizontal tube organism (O) and environment (E). The one in the middle will measure the mean level of tension (M). If you pour water into O it will be highest in that tube, lower in M and lowest in E—until all three are of the same level. The same would happen if water were first poured in tube E. Although factually you could pour water in tube M, in actual living, you cannot because tube M represents an operational abstraction, helpful for understanding the system O-E, but actually not existing.

An example from daily living may help to clarify further the meaning of tension and to detail the adequacy of organisms for environments and the adequacy of environments for organisms. At the end of a hard day's work, when I have become relaxedly fatigued, the mean level of tension of the system "waking organism-environment" sinks below the mean. The waking environment is no longer adequate for me, nor am I for it. The system goes through the phase of disintegrating, and reintegrates as "sleeping organism-environment" at a lower mean level of tension. I have "become " sleeping and am now "being" sleeping. I ate some salty food for supper and drank a lot of water. By 3 A.M. my bladder is quite distended. Stimuli from my bladder raise the level of tension in the sleeping system organism-environment which disintegrates, and reintegrates as the waking system organism-environment. I have become waking and am being waking as I empty my bladder. The mean level of tension in the waking environment now sinks below a mean. The waking system organism-environment now disintegrates and reintegrates as the sleeping system organism-environment. In this case the main source of stimuli prompting a change in the level of tension originated in the organism—i.e., in me. Loud street noises, my friend having a nightmare in the next room, or the restlessness of my dog beside my bed may be the main source of stimuli for my becoming waking. Provided I am not too disturbed by becoming waking, I will in time become sleeping again. We say my distended bladder, or honking horns in the street, awakened me. Those are spurious oversimplifications, expressions of unclear thinking about intricate natural phenomena.

SOURCES OF ANXIETY

Anxiety has sources. A stimulus felt as a threat to what has subjective value generates tension, which level exceeds the mean variation, cueing off anxiety. Anxiety appears whether what has subjective value is rational or irrational. This point has been elucidated in the two sets of anxiety dreams noted early in this paper. In the first set, illustrating sick anxiety, what had subjective value and was threatened was almost totally irrational. In the second large example, illustrating much less sick anxiety with more healthy components, what threatened was predominantly healthy and what was threatened, though sick, had some quite healthy components in it.

What is felt as a threat may originate in the organism or the environment, but it is the organism that evaluates the stimulus as a threat. When anxiety appears, we must ask what threatened and what was threatened. What threatened is always the exceeding of the mean variation of tension. But then we must ask what stimuli from within and/or from without generated the tension level change. What was threatened is always something in the organism that has subjective value, whether the individual is conscious or unconscious of the fact that he has felt threatened or knows what was threatened, or whether he knows how rational or irrational is his evaluation of what was threatened.

ATTITUDES TOWARD ANXIETY

Individuals vary in their attitudes toward anxiety. These attitudes may be more or less rational and irrational, and increase or decrease the intensity and extensity of the existing anxiety. These attitudes may increase or decrease the subjective feeling of anxiety. The intensity and extensity of objective anxiety may be more or less congruent with the subjective feeling of anxiety, or quite divergent. The subjective feeling may be maximal and objective evidence of anxiety minimal, or vice versa. A man's pupils may be widely dilated, his teeth chattering, palms wet, knees shaking and his face a picture of panic while he insists that he felt quite calm a minute before he fainted. To the extent that attitudes toward anxiety are more irrational, they will increase the speed of the cueing off of anxiety and its intensity, and will move the organism toward avoiding anxiety-prompting situations. This is an automatic, rigid or neurotic avoidance in which little rational choice is inherent. To the extent that attitudes toward anxiety are more rational, they will decrease the speed of the appearance of anxiety and its intensity, and will move the organism toward entering anxiety-prompting situations more frequently. This is a spontaneous, dynamic, or healthy moving into anxiety-prompting situations with freer choice. The measure of a creative person is his courage to enter with freer choice more anxiety situations and to do so more frequently. Self-realization of human creative potentialities is only possible through taking chances, through daring to leap into the unknown, to put at stake, and to threaten what has subjective value, rational and irrational.[13]

FUNCTIONS OF ANXIETY

Anxiety has functions. There is the natural one—i.e., through its existence it reminds the organism that the phase of disintegration has exceeded its mean limits. In each phase of disintegration there is evidence of the organism's being and becoming anxious. The phase of reintegration is the evidence of the resolution of that minimal phase of anxiety. Goldstein says there are minimal shocks to existence that happen to us from moment to moment.

Anxiety has rational and irrational functions. Irrationally, whether consciously or unconsciously it is used to intimidate others, to make them feel guilty. It is used aggressively to assert irrational claims on others for having prompted the anxiety and for making one feel so helpless. It is also used irrationally to justify avoiding situations which would threaten what has irrational value. Finally, it may be used for self-extinction through losing oneself in a sea of anxiety. In the service of such functions, the patterns of internally whipping it up, minimizing, exaggerating, and dramatizing are used.

An understanding of the irrational functions of irrational anxiety has been slow and painful. In a way, the history of psychoanalysis could be written from that perspective. The problems were pointedly brought to my awareness about fifteen years ago when I began to work with a woman who was severely depressed, massively abused, overwhelmingly anxious, morbidly dependent and severely resigned. The problems she presented had been and still are a challenge to psychoanalytic theory and therapy. Failures with such "masochistic" patients had been frequently reported in the literature; many analysts are still dubious about the accessibility of these people to therapy. Through Horney's contributions on masochism, sadism, morbid dependency, neurotic pride and self-hate, our understanding has deepened and our therapeutic effectiveness has increased.

In session after session this woman presented the picture I have described above. She kept repeating, "Help me. Do something," the while implying, "See how I suffer." That such patients suffer intensely there is no question. But this suffering is mainly neurotic. It has predominantly neurotic sources and serves neurotic purposes. They constantly and compulsively demand, and feel entitled to, relief. They seem incapable of tolerating temporarily increased suffering toward the objective of resolving the sources of their suffering.

My response to this woman's suffering, her anxiety and her productions was bewilderment, confusion, anxiety, and irritation. After a session I felt battered and bruised. From my work with her and with others presenting similar problems, as I availed myself of the help of more experienced colleagues, the literature on the subject and Horney's contributions, some clarification began to emerge.

I shall present more or less the sequence in which the problems involved became clearer to me. What follows is a composite of what was verbalized and what was implied by a variety of patients. The "Help me. Do something," mean, "I am so helpless. In fact, I am absolutely helpless. You are so strong. In fact, you are all-powerful. You are a magician. Because I am so helpless and you are so strong, I am entitled to your help. Also, because I am so helpless only a magician could help me. You have to be a magician and if you are not, my anxiety and suffering will become unbearable and it will be all your fault. When you accepted me as a patient you promised to help me. I am entitled to your help because I suffer so much and because I have no strength, no life in me. All strength, all life, all help are outside of me in you. If you do not help me and you are not using your magical powers for me, you are mean, cruel and heartless, and I am entitled to make you feel guilty and to make you suffer the way I suffer."

As the above became clearer and the anxiety and suffering abated, I began to catch glimpses of her in the waiting room and while walking into my office when she was unaware of being observed. I noted fleeting moments of relative relaxation, sometimes a smile and evidences of lessened anxiety and suffering. As soon as she caught my eye, or began talking, I could see the patterns of initiating and stirring up anxiety, of whipping it up, of exaggerating and dramatizing it. She was by now extremely anxious. Her attention was directed outward toward me and she was using her whole anxious being as a whip and a club on me. I now understood why I had felt bruised and battered. It also was clearer how she had used her anxiety to extort the help from me she felt I had and was withholding, and how she had used it to punish me.

As these patterns became less intense, other irrational functions of her anxiety became clearer, and the repetitive, bludgeoning complaint, "You don't understand me," that I heard from her and many others, became more understandable. I do not omit the fact that she was quite accurate in her statement that there was plenty I did not understand. But I began to note that it was when I felt I really had understood and been helpful that this assaultive type of response was forthcoming with increased anxiety, irritability and abused feelings. The meaning of "You don't understand me," began to emerge. I will use patient's words, actual and implied.

"You don't understand me and help me on my terms. You should take away my anxiety and my suffering without my making any effort in my own behalf, and justify my entitlement to all this help because my life has been so miserable and life has treated me so badly. You should affirm that I am all loving and pure and have been illtreated by a harsh world. But you should do all this in such a way that I do not become aware you are, or have helped me."

Only in recent years have I become more clearly aware of the awesome and awful neurotic dilemma these patients are in. Behind this absolute goodness and helplessness are an equally powerful self-sufficiency and a feeling of being all-knowing. So, the very help they genuinely need and neurotically demand is a threat to their neurotic need for self-sufficiency and their all-knowingness. And the well-known hurt-pride response is to restore pride by attacking. They must demolish you as the offender. Translated, "You don't understand me," says, "You have not helped me; I am not helpable because I am self-sufficient. You have not understood anything about me, because to admit you understood something about me that I did not, would be to admit I was not all-knowing, and that would be unbearable."

In my experience, when the need for self-sufficiency and the need to know begin to be deeply felt, other aspects of the expansive solution also come into the foreground, as well as many facets of resignation. As these are experienced, so is more of basic and central conflict. For these patients, this is a period of intense anxiety and suffering in their analysis. However, this suffering and anxiety are much more genuine and they bear with them more. More growing occurs. We see less and less of neurotic suffering and anxiety as such, and very little use of both for neurotic purposes.

Anxiety also functions to prompt patterns which attempt to deny and blot out the awareness of the existence of anxiety. Such patterns are the system of "shoulds," the process of alienating, externalizing, or automatic control of feelings, psychic fragmentation and denial through the supremacy of the mind.[16] Patterns which come into being to deny the subjective feeling of anxiety result in squelching the whole range of human feelings, but the objective evidence of anxiety and of other feelings continues, and may become more obvious, intensive and extensive.

ANXIETY AND THE PSYCHOPATHIC PROCESS

This is quite evident in people who manifest degrees of what I have called the psychopathic process.[17, 18] In its more flagrant form, it is referred to as the psychopathic personality. It has often been asserted that such people are not anxious. Such a statement is made on the limited criterion of reported subjective awareness of anxiety by the patient. I have had a long interest in and experience with such patients. I have yet to see one who was not anxious. All have shown various objective evidences of being anxious. Later in the work with them, their early reports that they did not feel anxious can be checked and relied on. In most instances they were not in fact aware of being anxious because they had squelched not only their feelings of being anxious, but almost the whole range of their feelings. As the work proceeds they do report awareness of fleeting moments of anxiety which they immediately squelched. Ultimately, they will tell you that there have been times when they were quite anxious but had denied that they were when asked. They had done so out of a neurotic need to maintain the illusion of being fearless, calm, imperturbable, strong and ruthless. By this time in our mutual work the criteria of subjective awareness and objective evidences of anxiety had been fulfilled. But anxious they were, often long before they were subjectively aware of it.

Rationally, anxiety functions to remind a healthier person that he is in a danger situation which he may or may not have recognized. It is a warning for him to evaluate his resources regarding the wisdom of chancing further anxiety which he feels he can tolerate, or of attempting a new direction of movement after a short retreat, or of leaving off his questing altogether to return to the fray at another time. Anxiety is a reminder to him to examine his tolerance for it at a particular time, so that he can determine whether he has not yet reached it, or exceeded it. With greater physical and psychological flexibility and toughness, the creative person can move into, stay in, hold himself in, and even rest in greater intensities and extensities of anxiety. Through such sequences he will become a stronger and deeper person, with greater human toughness and greater human compassion for himself and for others. This is not to suggest the welcoming of the pain of anxiety for pain's sake. This is a choosing of pain where it is foreknown and unavoidable, but with the hope of creative gain on the basis of previous similar experience.

ANXIETY—RATIONAL AND IRRATIONAL

Anxiety is more and less rational and irrational. When I speak of rational and irrational anxiety, I am referring to the proportions of existing anxiety. Anxiety is irrational to the extent that its sources, its functions and the attitudes toward it are irrational. And finally anxiety and being anxious are natural human experiences and human phenomena.

REFERENCES

1. Goldstein, K., *The Organism*, American Book Company, New York, 1939.
2. Horney, K., *Our Inner Conflicts*, W. W. Norton & Co., New York, 1945.
3. Horney, K., *Neurosis and Human Growth*, W. W. Norton & Co., New York, 1950.
4. Horney, *op. cit.*, note 2 above.
5. Horney, *op. cit.*, note 3 above.
6. Kelman, H., "Unitary Theory of Organism," presented in "The Meaning of Dreams," a course given at the American Institute for Psychoanalysis, Fall 1951, unpublished.
7. Angyal, A., *Foundations for a Science of Personality*, The Commonwealth Fund, New York, 1941.
8. *Ibid.*
9. Horney, *op. cit.*, note 3 above.
10. Whyte, L. L., *The Next Development in Man*, New American Library, 1951.
11. Goldstein, *op. cit.*, note 1 above.

12. Kelman, H., "Life History As Therapy," *The American Journal of Psychoanalysis*, XV, 2; XVI, 1; XVI, 2.
13. Kelman, H., "Rational and Irrational Authority," *The American Journal of Psychoanalysis*, XII, 1.
14. Goldstein, *op. cit.*, note 1 above.
15. *Ibid.*
16. Horney, *op. cit.*, note 3 above.
17. Kelman, H., "The Analytic Couch," *The American Journal of Psychoanalysis*, XIV, 1.
18. Kelman, *op. cit.*, note 12, XVI, 2.

The Body's Participation in Dilemma and Anxiety Phenomena

ALEXANDER R. MARTIN

At the Connecticut State Medical Society Symposium on Anxiety Conditions (1938), Dr. Edward F. Gildea made a statement that provides an appropriate text for this paper. "Disorders of almost any organ in the body may be due to deep-seated anxiety. Frequently the patient is not aware of the presence of anxiety in himself. The recognition and treatment of such patients constitutes one of the most intriguing problems of medicine."

This statement brings two questions to mind: "What is anxiety?" and "How does anxiety bring about somatic disorder?"

There is great need for simplification and clarification regarding the nature, extent, and intensity of the relationship between emotions and body changes. Emotions are nebulous, unlocalized, totally felt phenomena with certain physiological concomitants. In general, we may accept the idea that they can seriously disturb function or that they accompany, and are part of, disturbance of function. How-

Read before the Association for the Advancement of Psychoanalysis at the New York Academy of Medicine on March 28, 1945. Reprinted from *The American Journal of Psychoanalysis*, V, 1, 1945.

ever, if emotions are to be assigned a pathogenic role, then we must be more specific and more definite as to what we are talking about.

The definitions of anxiety given at the 1938 Symposium fail to give us anything consistent or specific. Dr. Eugene Kahn says: "Though emotionally the closest kin of fear, anxiety is characterized by the absence of the dreaded object, at least in the conscious part of the experience. It is this very absence of conscious content or object that makes anxiety the immensely threatening and shaking experience which it is." Dr. Gildea states: "Anxiety is an emotional experience in which the individual has the uneasy feeling of fear that something unpleasant or even terrible is going to happen." Dr. Terhune explains: "Anxiety is a prolonged psycho-physical reaction to fear. It is the normal reaction of the human organism to a past, present, or future threat, and the danger may be either real or fancied."

The *Dictionary of Psychology* offers this definition: "An emotional attitude or sentiment concerning the future characterized by an unpleasant alteration or mingling of dread and hope." In Freudian usage the term "anxiety" represents a combination of apprehension, of uncertainty and fear, with special reference to their bodily manifestations. Again according to Freud: "Anxiety functions as a signal of danger to the ego." [1]

Mittelmann and Wolff in "Emotions and Gastroduodenal Function" use "anxiety" to indicate "A reaction to danger in which defeat threatens, but in which resistance survives. It is commonly associated with hostility, resentment, guilt, and conflict." [2]

On careful study of all the above we find that some are describing the objective symptoms of anxiety, others, the subjective symptoms, and others the dynamics of anxiety.

Kubie feels that the confusion which has arisen over the psychoanalytic concept of anxiety rests perhaps on a triple category: "anxiety" as a symptom or finding, "anxiety" as a basic force, and "anxiety" as a disease process.[3]

Because of the enormous wealth of experience and material pertaining to this whole subject of emotions and bodily processes, I can focus on only one small area, an area which I think has significant value and provides a helpful meeting ground for psychoanalysis and psychosomatic medicine.

I propose to consider those bodily changes and emotions that accompany and are an integral part of the inner conflicts that beset human beings. I am not including whatever emotion may characterize conflict with the environment, but specifically the emotion that characterizes conflict within the individual, and/or conflicts that are set up within an individual when he is confronted with contradictory but equally important external situations. Finally, and most important, I am not thinking here of the emotions that may accompany unconscious conflicts, or that may accompany existing incompatible trends or feelings that are not in clear awareness. Rather, I am only considering the emotion that inevitably accompanies *emerging* conflicting trends or feelings; in other words, the emotion that inevitably accompanies the *imminent* awareness of inner conflict.

For the purpose of this paper, I am going to regard anxiety as that emotion with its physiological concomitants which always accompanies and is an integral part of *emergent* or *imminent* conflicts. In other words, let us agree here to regard anxiety as the characteristic emotion of two conflicting tendencies or feelings striving to find simultaneous conscious expression.

Whatever the feeling that accompanies these emerging conflicts, this feeling will always reach its maximum intensity at the imminence of a *dilemma,* that is, where the emerging contradictory trends are equally powerful.

Note that the mere existence of contradictory trends does not account for the development of anxiety. As long as the patient can keep contradictory trends apart, as long as these trends do not simultaneously enter consciousness, there is no anxiety. It is the approach of equally powerful contradictory trends to consciousness that represents the worst kind of a threat to the individual, the symptom of which, or the feeling tone accompanying which, could be referred to as dilemma anxiety. Horney says: "By far the greatest part of manifest anxiety is the result of being helplessly caught in a dilemma, both sides of which are imperative." [4]

In my opinion we get different degrees of anxiety according to whether a conflict or a dilemma approaches consciousness. We must not try to deal with basic conflicts at the outset. The derivatives and attenuations of conflict or dilemma must first be brought to awareness. Only after this has been accomplished do the basic conflicts themselves become accessible.

The approach of incompatible trends to consciousness —and I mean, of course, imperative incompatible trends —creates a need for relief. Such approach may be sudden or gradual. External situations, objects, or persons of special significance to the patient activate an unconscious conflict, bring it closer to awareness, and perhaps set up an imminent dilemma. The patient will react in many ways. There may be actual physical detachment or escape from the situation, detachment through alcohol or drugs or induced emotional detachment. There may be a radical change in the manner of living. There may be psychotic solution, or there may be somatic solution, that is, solution through body participation.

Because the approach of a dilemma to consciousness gives rise to the most serious anxiety, this is most likely in my opinion to result in perceptible and extensive expression in bodily processes. The body as a whole participates in the imminent dilemma and gives rise to a contradictory clinical picture which will be mentioned later. Then, in certain individuals or under certain circumstances the whole or a part of the body may participate in a solution or an attempt at a solution.

In *New Ways in Psychoanalysis* Horney mentions the ship's officer who must give an order to change the course of his ship to avoid immediate collision. If at that moment his hand or voice fails to function, he would be thrown into a panic which is "exactly comparable to the neurotic's anxiety." [4] Here is an opportunity to clarify my opinion as to the relationship between dilemma, anxiety, and body participation. Horney indicates that because the officer's hand failed him he was thrown into a panic. My thought would be that the failure of the hand to function at that particular moment would be the somatic solution of a dilemma and that the panic was the whole being's expression of the dilemma and did not follow it. He was, in other words, a neurotic ship's officer, one of whose conflicts had to do with giving and receiving orders. A well-integrated man, relatively free from inner dilemma would not have anxiety or lose his head if his hand was shot or injured at such a critical moment.

Horney adds, "An inhibition about making decisions, for example, is not in itself contingent to anxiety, but it will tend to that result if it cannot be overcome in a crucial moment." Here I would say everything hinges around the phenomenon of the crucial moment. For many neurotics almost every situation is a crucial moment. The complete inability to make decisions accompanies and does not cause the anxiety and as such is a symptom or expression of the dilemma. That is, equally powerful contradictory trends or attitudes or feelings are trying to find expression simultaneously. This is the worst possible threat to the individual and produces intolerable feelings from which the individual must seek to escape.

The need to distinguish between conflict and dilemma and the relation of maximum anxiety to dilemma are shown clearly in the common dream of being chased. When nothing interferes with your running in the dream, the emotion is relatively mild, and you are less likely to wake up. This dream dramatizes a somewhat uneven conflict. On the other hand when strenuous efforts are made to run, and your feet are leaden, you feel held back, and you make no headway whatever, then excruciating anxiety results and you frequently wake up rigid in a cold sweat with tachycardia and pallor. A similar nightmare occurs when you try to cry out and cannot. Such dreams are dramatizations of serious dilemmas within yourself.

A series of dreams from a patient gives a clear picture of the dramatization of conflicts and dilemmas. In his early life this patient had dreams in which he was chased by buffaloes. He was always unable to run and invariably woke up in a panicky, terror-stricken state. This dream later changed. He was still being chased by buffaloes but now he would throw himself down on the ground and let the buffaloes ride over him. From these dreams he did not awake. Another variant of this buffalo dream occurred around the same time or a little later. He was still being chased by buffaloes but just as they reached him he would take off and fly over their heads. From these dreams he did not awake. The first dream expressed a definite dilemma, and the subsequent dreams show his attempts at solution which apparently were sufficiently satisfactory to avoid acute panic, that is, to avoid imminent awareness. The solution dreams expressed his behavior in life. In his own words he said that he allowed people to ride over him. He always effaced and humiliated himself and let others have the upper hand. The other way of dealing with life, which he felt was overwhelming him, was to detach himself, to show indifference—in his own words: "I felt I could rise above getting involved in petty bickering."

The foregoing has dealt with what I consider to be the principal dynamics of anxiety. They explain the subjective symptoms of anxiety which have so often been described, and which are experienced in classical form in the above type of nightmare. There is anxiety when the patient complains of varying degrees of apprehension, helplessness, inescapability, "something awful going to happen." Conflicts can approach consciousness slowly or suddenly and this would be felt subjectively as slowly increasing, or sudden apprehension, with feelings of helplessness and incapacity. The more the emerging conflict has the character of a dilemma, the less the individual is able to express his thoughts and feelings clearly, and the more the objective picture becomes one of tension, trembling, immobility —which are the classic symptoms of acute panic.

Further examination of patients with this subjective and objective picture of severe anxiety shows evidence of a physiological or somatic dilemma involving the total individual. Unless a solution or a compromise takes place, such a dilemma actually seriously threatens the entire internal and metabolic economy of the individual.

The objective findings of panic, which show involvement of the total individual in a dilemma, are the following: the entire voluntary musculature shows simultaneous contraction of flexor and extensor systems. The clash of opposing trends is clearly reflected in a diencephalic conflict or thalamic disequilibrium. We find the entire body flooded with adrenalin which it does not utilize. There is pallor, facial contortion, profuse sweating, tachycardia, high blood pressure, but without any elevation whatever in blood sugar and there is a definite alkalosis. The dilemma is also reflected in the vegetative nervous system where we find simultaneous activation of both the sympathetic and the cranio-autonomic divisions.

There are contradictory, inconsistent findings in the gastro-duodenal tracts of patients under definite anxiety stress. There is, according to Mittelmann and Wolff,[2] hypomotility and hyposecretion with some, and hypermotility and hypersecretion with others, which can be reconciled if we postulate a dilemma involving the total organism. Still others emphasize spastic phenomena throughout the entire gastrointestinal tract.

A relation between severe anxiety and dilemma could explain the paradoxical behavior of certain patients with severe hypoglycaemia. They are restless, irritable, apprehensive, and wear an agonized anxious expression; they are consciously and violently opposed to taking any sugar whatever although their body is crying aloud for it. This is a typical anxiety nightmare situation. The one substance that would bring relief is violently rejected. There is evidence that the convulsions of the hypoglycaemic, like other convulsions, may be some kind of dilemma phenomena. The classical convulsive seizure passes from tonic to clonic spasm. The clonus expresses the rapidly fluctuating struggle between the two opposing forces, which in the beginning had completely deadlocked the individual. Clonus thus represents the body's attempt to relieve a massive dilemma.

The relationship between anxiety, dilemma, and pathology is by no means a new or revolutionary idea. However, because the whole subject has not been carefully thought through, there has been a tendency for those interested in the role of emotions in disease to think of anger, sorrow, grief, rage, resentment, and other normal emotions as potentially pathogenic. The excellent work of Wolff and Mittelmann [2] is being cited as proof that rage, anger, resentment, etc. can cause peptic ulcer and other gastrointestinal pathology. This is a gross misinterpretation and is only half the story. These emotions *per se* are not responsible for bodily disorders or dysfunction, although the authors themselves have applied to them the term "destructive emotions" which I am sure they would now refute. The body is equipped to develop and express rage, resentment, fear, grief, etc., and when these emotions are intense and find expression, we get an exaggerated physiological picture. It is when a strong conflict occurs over the expression of these emotions that we get a pathological condition. Snowden says, "nature intended all emotion to lead to physical activity immediately. When this does not occur, the blood is poisoned. Often two schoolboys fight and then shake hands and are friends. If prevented from fighting they cannot be friends. It is a true statement when people thenceforth say 'there is bad blood between them!' "

But these pathological conditions must not be attributed to so-called "repression of emotions." This term is too one-sided and static in its implication. Nor is the real state of affairs or source of trouble to be seen as "pent-up hate," or "pent-up grief," or "pent-up anger." What prevents expression of feelings and causes dilemma is not merely a block, but another trend of an opposite nature trying to find simultaneous expression. Trouble arises for example when a powerful tendency to express defiance or rage is met at the same time by an equally powerful tendency to comply and submit. Viewing the patient dynamically, we realize that each trend is active and checking the other, and, therefore, each deserves equal attention when we come to consider cause and treatment.

Because dilemma anxiety is so intolerable, the total personality consciously and unconsciously uses every means in its power to solve it or to find some compromise.

The most serious dilemmas in our culture occur in connection with showing feelings. It is the soldier who is beset by a strong inclination to show fear and run and an equally strong desire to hold his ground, who later develops anxiety neurosis. Anxiety is produced when the tendency to express grief conflicts with the need to maintain a bold front. The stoical, courageous woman who "never lets go" at her husband's death, but carries on so wonderfully has already set up an anxiety condition.

If subjective feelings of great uneasiness, helplessness, emptiness, and impending disaster which accompany an imminent serious dilemma, do not find verbal expression, but are held back because of some equally strong tendency to maintain poise and equanimity, then a further conflict is created, more anxiety is produced, and a vicious circle is set up. Regarding this, Gildea states: "There are those who find expression of anxiety through verbal, or external and motor channels difficult or impossible. For these patients outlets are found through the vegetative nervous system and ultimately in the direction of one or more visceral organs. Such disturbances, while similar to those associated with emotional disturbances in general such as fear, differ in that physiological response is rarely as general and profound."

When Gildea speaks of anxiety finding an outlet in some visceral organ, he implies a kind of mechanistic and haphazard short-circuiting. It is important to realize that physical symptoms following a period of anxiety may represent a kind of figurative, symbolic attempt to solve the dilemma, to reach some compromise that will satisfy both trends and thus relieve the anxiety. For example, hysterical paralysis of the arm can be one way of solving a dilemma connected with striking someone upon whom the patient is dependent. Globus hystericus represents a compromise for a dilemma connected with swallowing insults and the impulse to retaliate, or a dilemma connected with accepting and rejecting. Hypermetropia, or farsightedness, may be a somatic solution of a dilemma related to a fear of getting close to anybody or getting close to reality. Diarrhea may be a somatic symbolic attempt to resolve a dilemma connected with "letting go" or relieving feelings. Similarly, constipation may be the somatic solution of a dilemma connected with holding on to something. Those two inseparables in adolescence, constipation and acne, in the great majority of instances are not causally related at all, but represent the body's participation in one and the same dilemma solution, a dilemma connected with retention and withholding. Where constipation and acne are part of the same somatic pattern, attempts to cure the acne by relieving the constipation with laxatives, which is the usual procedure, are very likely to aggravate the acne.

Dizziness and falling I have found related to dilemmas connected with facing disillusionment, having to accept facts, coming down from heights, coming down to earth. Fainting I have seen as a somatic way of resolving dilemmas connected with effacing oneself.

Each symptom has a purpose. Obviously unless we do something about the basic dilemma by working with its derivatives and attenuations, the removal of one somatic symptom may be followed by somatic symptoms elsewhere, or by a return of the actual anxiety dilemma with severe subjective symptoms. We have all noticed in the extremely tense, anxious patient, that when a physical symptom or disturbance of function develops, the anxiety is immediately lessened. This would indicate that a compromise, or dilemma solution has taken place at a somatic level.

Consider the above mentioned paralyzed arm. Treatment of such a patient by trying to convince him that there are no organic origins of such a paralysis, and that the trouble is "nervous," "functional," or "mental," may be followed by a return of the subjective anxiety. A patient of mine with severe anxiety felt great relief when she developed a stutter. She made no effort to relieve this stutter and resisted all attempts to cure her. In another instance, a well-meaning physician demonstrated to a hypochondriacal man that his basal metabolic rate was normal and that he was in good physical health; the patient thereupon developed severe depression anxiety with fear of impending death. One patient of mine under circumstances which had previously produced migraine attacks is now completely free of them, but she complains of apprehension, uneasiness, "feeling terrible," and "feeling like two people."

We see in all of this one explanation for the tenacity

with which the hypochondriacal patient clings to and defends his organic symptoms despite negative findings and the advice and opinion of scores of specialists.

Physicians must come to consider anxiety just as they would body temperature and regard it as a measure of the degree and imminence of conflict within every person. There is some anxiety present in all of us from time to time because the inconsistent and contradictory demands of family and social life create inner conflicts and dilemmas. Relationships with diametrically opposite parents and grandparents are a source of conflict and anxiety. The feeling that accompanies everyday conflict has some positive, dynamic value because it is by that feeling that we are moved to find a way out, to reach a compromise in our psychosomatic life and/or in our social life.

In contrast to the older Freudian instinctivistic theories, dilemmas and anxieties of pathogenic intensity are now felt to be solely derived or formed from incompatible compulsive trends that the individual was forced to adopt in childhood because of a hostile early environment. For many individuals with incompatible compulsive tendencies, certain periods in life bring the trends closer to consciousness with consequent anxiety. For instance, there is at puberty the dilemma between the opposing trends of growing up and remaining adolescent; at the involutional period there are dilemmas connected with loss of procreative function and growing old. It is always the meaning of life situations to each individual that brings such conflicts closer to consciousness, and thus produces the anxiety. Whether we can carry on through life's vicissitudes and maintain our personal relationships without undue dilemma and anxiety depends upon our upbringing and our preparation for living.

How the meaning of a situation determines a serious anxiety dilemma is shown from the following: a woman had intense pain in the solar plexus region, with sinking feelings, palpitation and shortness of breath, and the feeling that something terrible was going to happen. She said this happened whenever she stooped over. I found that it only occurred when she bent over the crib to look after her baby, not when she touched her toes during morning exercise or when she bent over to make the bed. The responsibility of the baby aroused opposing trends connected with wishing to be free and irresponsible, and at the same time to maintain high ethical standards, also with desiring to possess and to dominate on the one hand, and to be possessed and dominated on the other. For several months this woman had run the gamut of specialists to determine whether or not she had heart trouble or stomach trouble.

A recognition of the role of dilemma in those acute anxiety states which call for immediate treatment will provide us with a rationale for a more intelligent use of sedative drugs. Since the total organism is always involved in every dilemma, it is possible to relieve some of the physiological involvement. Drugs obviously do not remove the dilemma.

While we are thus reducing an acute anxiety, we are mainly concerned to learn the direction that will be taken by nature to solve the dilemma anxiety and attempt a cure. As has been indicated, the patient may quite unconsciously find a way out in his social life—alcoholism, drug addiction, increased sociability, increased isolation, detachment, increased sexuality, impotence, homosexuality, masturbation. Our first inclinations should be to go along with these symptoms and help the patient to accept them as having some function in diminishing his dilemma and anxiety. For a patient who gradually or suddenly becomes

impotent or beset with homosexual longings or an excessive desire to masturbate, it is very reassuring to realize
that these are symptoms and not causes of his trouble. They
are strategies and experimentations unconsciously carried
out which bring temporary relief from anxiety, but which
are followed by a still more complex and intense dilemma.

We have to make some distinction on the one hand between the body's participation in the imminent dilemma,
that is, the bodily phenomena that accompany subjective
symptoms of great apprehension, helplessness, weakness;
and on the other hand, the body's participation in the
solution or compromise. As has been indicated, when the
body participates in a compromise solution of a dilemma
this often coincides with a disappearance of the subjective
symptoms.

One such patient wanted to be in touch with me. She
had difficulty over what was aroused by the perceptual experience of the analytic hour but her feelings about me
she could not express, so she made remote contact many
times over the telephone. While she wanted to be with me
she also kept drawing farther back. Finally she drank to
the point of not remembering what she was doing and then
she telephoned me. Now she had contact, but at the same
time she remained unaware.

One patient's posture on the analytic couch, and particularly the position of her legs, indicated body participation in a dilemma. Her legs were very tense and slightly
flexed, and not crossed but tightly held together as if in
a spasm. The particular dilemma or conflict expressing
itself here had to do with more free self-expression and
opening up in analysis. She had a dream during this period
of climbing a hill, and she saw a girl sitting on a rock some
way up the hill who had her legs wide open, exposing

herself, as the patient said, "in a disgusting fashion." In analysis this patient was afraid to open up; she was afraid not only of what the analyst would learn about her but what she would learn about herself. There was all the time a compulsion to open up but also great concern about being rejected. In another patient there was a very decided feeling that she was constipated, yet she actually had diarrhea. Again, we see body participation in the dilemma proper in severe stutterers. In accessory movements of the head and upper part of the body which accompany the effort to talk, there is obviously a simultaneous action of opposing groups of muscles, which almost reaches the spasm point. There is a rapid fluctuation in the actual stutter of an aggression-recession dilemma.

One patient had severe anxiety and depression with no physical concomitants. On her return from a weekend at home during the course of treatment she developed a stutter which coincided with the disappearance of her depression and anxiety. This we can think of as body participation in a solution. Following a period of anxiety, a patient may begin to develop physical signs or symptoms that are anomalous and non-specific, or that may conform to a definite organic disease. When this occurs the victim's subjective symptoms often disappear. We should remember that any physical pattern following a period of even mild apprehension, and *usually displacing such apprehension,* may be a symbolic way out of such a dilemma—that is, an attempt at cure just as any other symptom or sign in the body, such as inflammation, is an attempt at cure. Many of the conversion symptoms in hysteria represent somatic compromises or solutions of conflict. This seems to be particularly evident in instances of functional paralysis, either muscular or sensory in type. Functional blindness is obviously a way out of a dilemma connected with seeing something. One patient, a writer, who had severe headaches and went through a severe bout of drinking, realized that something was worrying him. At this point in the analysis and in his writing, there was a dilemma about whether to write his book in the third person or the first person. It was obviously a dilemma about getting closer to himself and to other people. At home he remembered that this matter had come up in the analysis and his headache had immediately begun to disappear. He began to write in the first person and changed what he had already written into the first person, and with this his headache left him.

There is the whole complex subject of the genesis of those psychobiological characteristics that favor or facilitate the participation of the body in conflicts and in their solution. A great deal of research is being done along this line. I can only suggest certain avenues of approach that I feel very strongly are worth exploring. One has as its starting point a re-examination of the theory of the function of the central nervous system as held by Pavlov,[5] Sherrington,[6] Freud,[1] and the late nineteenth century neurologists and psychiatrists, and especially their interpertation of what is known as the "startle state" or "startle pattern." This "startle pattern" is the first manifestation of reflex behavior by the new born infant as described by Moro,[7] Landis,[8] and Hunt, and summarized by Dewey.[9] Pavlov, Freud, Sherrington did not see that integration was primary, but rather they looked upon this fundamental form of behavior, that is, the "startle state," as "the product of a primitive explosion." "A diffuse, relatively patternless uncoordinated irradiation of excitatory processes." It is spoken of as "more basic and primitive than organized action." This school of thought believes that organized responses are carved out of the "startle state" largely by superimposition of patterns of organized inhibitions. Thus these authorities postulate innate inevitable basic conflicts within the organism—a fundamental duality, an inner conflict between excitatory and inhibitory processes. Pavlov's inhibitory process becomes a mechanism of defense against primitive diffused irradiation of excitation which produces the "startle state."

These authorities, and I quote Pavlov, believe the function of the central nervous system is "directed *toward* unification, integrating the work of all parts of the organism." Their whole theoretical structure is built on the belief that individuation precedes integration.

But all of this is in complete disagreement with the fact now definitely established by modern embryology [10] that integration precedes individuation. Primarily the organism is integrated, and the earliest responses are totally integrated responses. Effective local action finally evolves from elimination of all other movements that are no longer essential. The "startle state," far from being diffuse and purposeless, is an early purposive and integrated response which through experience will become more and more refined by the elimination of elements that are no longer necessary. Thus the central nervous system acts to conserve energy and improve efficiency. It does not start out with explosive unorganized and undifferentiated primitive action that has to be controlled and tamed. In the healthy organism there is no conflict between higher and lower centers, but cooperation and coordination directed towards greater and greater efficiency. For instance, the immediate reaction of a very young puppy to a sound is to move the whole body in the direction of that sound. While this is massive, it is totally integrated, organized movement. As time, experience, and education go on there is elimination of the unnecessary elements of this totally integrated response until the final reactions are refined down to the minimal essentials for detection of that sound under the prevailing circumstances—so that, ultimately, the most highly specialized reaction might be the simple pricking of one ear.

The older school, in the case of this puppy, would believe that response and movement first began in the system of reflexes related to the hearing function which would produce the local pricking of the ear as the primary response but then because of the *immature development of inhibition,* excitation immediately spreads to the rest of the animal, giving rise to massive, uncoordinated, purposeless movements.

The conceptions of Pavlov and Sherrington found their greatest expressions in the Freudian philosophy, which presented man always at war with his instincts. It gave us the life and death instincts and referred to the malignancy of one's own instincts, all of which is well epitomized in Menninger's book, *Man Against Himself.*

However, the whole idea that inner conflict is our inevitable, permanent heritage and is primary and fundamental, we can subscribe to no longer. There must accordingly be a radical change in our whole approach to the behavior of the organism.

More and more proof is forthcoming to support Horney's assertion that those drives which have hitherto been regarded as instinctive, innate, and inborn, and the basis for all the conflicts that cause neurosis, are acquired, compulsive drives; drives that the individual was forced to adopt in early life because of deficiencies and/or malevolence in the attitudes of the parents.

Specifically, I would say that parental attitudes such as neglect, rejection, exploitation, possessive love, over-protection, and particularly, broken, unpredictable homes and inconsistent, erratic discipline, are unquestionably the strongest factors in initiating and in paving the way for conflicting drives and feelings and pathogenic dilemmas. These compulsive drives, while originating in the family life, are unconsciously perpetuated by an insensitive culture and later by the individual himself. This insensitive culture often includes the family physician who is not thinking of the causes, signs, and symptoms of inner conflict, and how the child is trying to solve it. He is likely to deal with all physical phenomena somewhat superficially without realizing that the younger the child the more the body will participate as a whole in dealing with both his outer and his inner conflicts.

We have to ask: why is it that with some patients, conflicts and dilemmas are expressed and solved somatically, while in others they do not find expression through the body at all? This question must be answered because those who make use of their body, or those whose bodies for some reason or other participate in the conflict, do not as a rule pass on to the more serious psychoses. Temper tantrums, generalized spastic tensions and convulsive phenomena, breath holding, etc., do not feature so much in the early history of schizophrenia, but do so much more in the early history of psychopathic personality and psychoneurosis. Temper tantrums in particular are a feature of psychopathic early history.

That body participation is in some way or another an insurance against the more serious inaccessible psychoses has long been known. Also, it is known that body participation relieves the subjective symptoms of anxiety.

In my opinion, further study of the relationship between body participation, dilemma, and anxiety would provide some explanation of the following:

(1) There is more physical illness in the life-history of the general population than in the life-history of the mental hospital population; and the most severe psychotic, that is the schizophrenic, suffers least from physical illness in his lifetime and has the fewest surgical operations in the mental hospital population.

(2) There is a higher incidence of surgical operations in the lifetime of the general population than in the lifetime of the mental hospital populations.[11] The highest incidence of surgical operations is found in the life-history of psychopathic personalities who are the least psychotic or closest to the "normal." Then in every mental hospital we have those dramatic instances of individuals with chronic severe psychoses, regarded as incurable, showing recovery or remarkable improvement after some serious physical illness or accident.

Finally we come to the convulsive and shock treatment of psychoses. It would seem that any consideration of the rationale of this new shock and convulsive treatment must take into account some of the factors above mentioned. As I have said, schizophrenics show the least body participation, but we know that with them conflicts and dilemmas are resolved mostly by a kind of detachment or withdrawal. It seems significant, therefore, that shock and convulsive treatment is most effective in those schizophrenics who show some tendency to use their body, that is, in the catatonic who is regarded as the most suitable for convulsive treatment. Also the treatment is effective on those schizophrenics with lively affect, or, in other words, those who are showing their feelings, also with those who are stuporous; whereas the young hebephrenic shows the poorest response to shock therapy.

One patient of mine had apprehension, uneasiness, feelings of unreality and inadequacy with depression. He was convinced he was doomed. He ran the gamut of doctors and one decided to give him a few shock treatments. He was given six and after these the depression lifted considerably; but he then had marked tensions beginning in his head and migrating to different parts of his body. Despite, or perhaps because of, these tensions, he had a more hopeful attitude toward himself. Where previously he had had feelings of unreality and depersonalization, and had felt that nothing could be done about it, he now became interested in studying his life history to know more about himself. He always said he got "insight after the shock."

In the various body participations we can always look for attempts at cure. In attempting to deal with a dilemma or conflict, the body will first act as a whole. At first children naturally will attempt to deal with every conflict situation rather massively in the same way as they naturally deal with life in a massive but integrated fashion. Under circumstances where this natural massive physical expression of tendencies and feelings has been discouraged and ridiculed, and where the parental demands have been to replace natural physical muscular bodily activity with reasoning and intellectual activities, this may block the way, or render it difficult for the body to participate in a conflict.

Understanding of what determines body participation involves consideration of all those factors that have operated in giving the young child a concept of its body. The extensive and intensive work of Paul Schilder [12] in this connection has particular value. We have to consider to what extent the child acquires a clear concept of his body through a wide variety of opportunities for using it in frequent contact with personal and impersonal reality. Consider in this connection the individual brought up by detached parents who unconsciously reject and show an unwillingness and a strong antipathy to touch or handle the child. Such a child will not have the same concept of his body as the child who has been frequently handled, whether roughly or affectionately, and who has had many experiences of physical contact with human beings. Certainly the rough and tumble play, like young puppies in a basket, which all young children, boys and girls, love to indulge in, provides an important and essential experience for learning about the body in relation to others. It is this type of play which modern civilization, particularly in cities, provides no opportunity for, and it is the type of play which is particularly subject to disapproval.

There is certainly a very important relationship between the development of the body concept and the evolution of language—especially radical metaphor, idiom and figurative language. As has been noted, some patients are constantly expressing their dilemmas in some figurative way through body processes. Certainly many dreams [13] are dramatizations of figures of speech. That the development of language is closely linked with body structure and function is shown by the fact that between sixty to seventy per cent of idiomatic phrases and figurative speech in the English language derives from some structure or function of the human body.

The following restatement, I realize, is highly controversial, but whatever interest and argument it may provide should lead to a clearer understanding of the relationship between conflict, anxiety, and body participation.

The contributions of Freud, Pavlov, and Sherrington were based upon the theory that totally integrated action or behavior was a resultant or ultimate process rather than the original and primary characteristic of the organism; that is, they believed that the part always acted or responded before the whole organism. These dualistic or pluralistic philosophies presuppose a constitutional stage permanently set for conflict and dilemma phenomena. Adherence to a holistic point of view refutes any such innate basis for fundamental inner conflict or dilemma. Thinking holistically, structure and function becomes structure *in* function, individual *and* environment becomes individual *in* environment. In physics, mass and energy becomes mass *in* energy. Under a fourth dimensional holistic point of view, male and female, right and left, light and dark, past and present are relative and can never be fundamental bases, but can only be acquired bases for inner conflict.

The man who lives holistically, who has, as it were, a "stake in the universe," and a sense of being a unique but integral part of the human family, is one who has not had to repress his inner conflicts. He is, I think, the *Homo Dei* Thomas Mann describes in "The Magic Mountain" as the "lord of counterpositions." [14] He possesses inner conflicts but is not possessed by them.

The body becomes involved pathologically in conflicts that are repressed. It is through feeling and admitting into awareness our total involvement in conflict that we not only obviate such pathology but promote body functioning and our creative functioning with others.

REFERENCES

1. Freud, S., *New Introductory Lectures on Psychoanalysis*, W. W. Norton & Co., New York, 1933.
2. Mittelmann, B. and Wolff, H. G., "Emotions and Gastroduodenal Function," *Psychosomatic Medicine,* IV, 2, 1942.
3. Kubie., L. S., "A Physiological Approach to the Concept of Anxiety," *Psychosomatic Medicine,* III, 3, 1941.
4. Horney, K., *New Ways in Psychoanalysis,* W. W. Norton & Co., New York, 1939.
5. Pavlov, I. P., *Conditioned Reflexes and Psychiatry,* International Publishers, New York, 1941.
6. Sherrington, C. S., *The Integrative Action of the Nervous System,* Yale University Press, New Haven, 1926.
7. Moro, E., *"Das Erste Trimenon,"* Munch. med. Wschr., 65:1147, 1918.
8. Landis, C. and Hunt, W. A., *The Startle Pattern,* Farrar & Rinehart, Inc., New York, 1939.
9. Dewey, E., *Behavior Development in Infants,* Columbia University Press, New York, 1935.
10. Coghill, G. E., "The Neuro-Embryologic Study of Behavior. Principles, Perspective and Aim," *Science,* 78, August 18, 1933.
11. Martin, A. R., "The Incidence of Surgical Operations in the Life Histories of One Thousand Women Admitted to Sheppard and Enoch Pratt Hospital," M.D. Thesis 1933, Queen's University of Belfast.
12. Schilder, P., *The Image and Appearance of the Human Body,* "Psyche" Monograph No. 4, Kegan Paul, Trench and Trubner, 1935.
13. Schilder, P., "The Body Image in Dreams," *Psychoanalytic Review* No. 29, 1942.
14. Mann, T., *The Magic Mountain,* Alfred A. Knopf, New York, 1927.

Some Aspects of Sex in Neuroses

FREDERICK A. WEISS

Our understanding of the role of sex in neuroses has
grown with the development of our modern view of
nature and man. The old, compartmentalizing view which
in biology as well as in psychology separated body and
mind, and special functions from the total function, and
which attempted to explain the whole on the basis of its
parts, has had to be replaced by the holistic approach. This
approach sees the organism as a whole whose partial functions—for example, the sexual one—are determined by its
total function. The individual is seen as an integrated
mind-body unit, which in turn forms a part of the greater
unit: the surrounding culture.

The holistic approach is particularly necessary in dealing
with the problem of sex which, in addition to the genital
end organ, involves the endocrine, vascular and nervous
systems. The integrated functioning of these systems is
determined by the total personality. While the sexual behavior of lower animals is determined exclusively by hor-
mones, sexual behavior in man is relatively independent

Read before the Association for the Advancement of Psychoanalysis
at the New York Academy of Medicine on May 24, 1950. Reprinted
from *The American Journal of Psychoanalysis*, X, 1, 1950.

of hormonal influences. Experiences and emotions, which often strongly influence the hormonal level and the hormonal functions, take the decisive place.

The static, mechanistic concept of physical, as well as psychic, processes has also had to be replaced by the dynamic theory of total interaction between changeable molecules and atoms, with resulting qualitative changes. The individual is no longer seen as an isolated, unchangeable body whose emotional life consists in shifting a quantity of energy—for example, of love or sex—from a subject, A, to an object, B. Man functions as a more or less integrated whole in dynamic interaction with others. The role played by sex is governed by the emotional dynamics prevailing in his total interpersonal relationships. However, we have also come to recognize that not even the newly established units in both systems—the atom in the world of the universe and the self in the world of man—constitute final "atomi," unstructured, indivisible entities. Both the atom and the self have been found to possess a significant inner structure and to harbor strong energies whose release can result in constructive or destructive action.

THE HOLISTIC APPROACH

Freud saw the coexistence of sexual disorders and neurotic disturbances. But, under the impact of Darwin's instinct theory, he considered disturbances of the sexual instinct the *cause* of neuroses. He said in his autobiography: "I was led into regarding the neuroses as being without exception disturbances of the sexual function, the so-called 'actual' neuroses being the direct toxic expression of such disturbances and the psychoneuroses their mental expression."

Freud saw actual neuroses, among which he included anxiety neuroses, neurasthenia, and hypochondriasis, as caused by toxemia due to arbitrarily impaired sexual function. As the most common etiological factors he mentioned the practice of coitus interruptus, excessive masturbation and sexual abstinence. "The symptoms of these patients," Freud wrote, "are not mentally determined or removable by analysis . . . they must be regarded as direct toxic consequences of disturbed sexual chemical processes." [1] This early theory of Freud's has never been modified, although it leaves unanswered the problem of *why* the victims of actual neuroses had not developed a normal sexual life.

Today it appears self-evident that excessive masturbation, compulsive sexual abstinence and coitus interruptus have to be considered as *symptoms* of severe anxiety and deep inner conflicts. They *can* be treated successfully by analysis if we understand their meaning and their dynamics. We must start by asking what might have prevented the patient from establishing a healthier pattern in his sexual life and from desiring and obtaining a fuller, more realistic satisfaction.

Is it a fear or rejection of sex? Is it an unconscious fear of the partner, or a repressed hostility against him, an unrecognized competition with him? Is it the fear of losing control? Is it a result of a disturbed relationship of the patient to himself: neurotic pride, which makes the partner appear "not good enough," or self-contempt, which leads the patient to feel unworthy of the sexual relationship? Is he afraid of the test situation which the sexual act may represent for him? Is he blocked by a conscious or unconscious devaluation of sex? Does he fear the responsibilities which may arise out of the relationship with a real partner? Does he sense some danger to the idealized image which has formed of himself as the perfect partner, the inexhaustible super-male, the irresistible lover?

The mere listing of all these diagnostic possibilities indicates the only constructive approach to these sexual difficulties: *the analysis of the total character structure of the patient.* This character structure cannot be explained by the development of one of its aspects: sex—even sex conceived of in the enlarged sense of Freudian libido. Character—from the Greek *charassein,* to engrave—is the engraved life pattern. It grows in dialectical interaction between the total individual and the total environment.

Man is not only a biological organism, but also a social individual functioning within the greater whole of his culture. In the process of character analysis, apparently unchangeable "biological" and universal attitudes with regard to sex ("penis envy," "Oedipus complex," etc.) reveal themselves as changeable, culturally fostered and neurotic. Our culture, characterized by a conflicting attitude towards sex which combines elements of devaluation of sex with overemphasis on sex, often reinforces conflicts about sex.

Even quantitative variations of the sexual function, as recorded in Kinsey's figures on "sexual outlets," are only symptoms which reflect the role sex plays in the total character structure. Sex, like drinking, eating and sleeping, constitutes a vital need. This need not only varies in intensity with the individual constitution and the presence or absence of other satisfactions, it is also strongly influenced by unconscious factors, such as anxiety or neurotic drives.[2] This holds true for both minus and plus variations.

"Can a woman really enjoy sex?" was the surprised question of a patient who had been taught by her mother that sex is a necessary evil, to be used for social climbing and to be performed only as a marital duty.

"I have a dislike for fussing around down there," said a woman extremely proud of her intellect, by which she tried to control her life. To her, "down there" meant something beneath and outside her personality, which of course would never participate in the sexual act.

The patient who tells us, "My sex drive is extremely strong," usually ascribes the intensity of his sexual needs to his innate temperament or his freedom from conventional taboos. Often he is filled with conscious or unconscious pride which is supported by the fact that in our culture a strong sex drive is still mistaken for evidence of real strength, of "strong masculinity." But anxiety and inner conflict often provide the extra charge for the patient's feelings. Here sex assumes the function of a sedative. Overemphasis on sex as a cultural phenomenon occurs at times during which anxiety and tension permeate public life, the prospect for full and constructive living appears poor and the real meaning of life seems to be lost. Where life as a whole seems futile, sex may become an overevaluated substitute, a tranquilizer, a stimulant to overcome a feeling of inner emptiness.

Similarly, in the individual patient overemphasis on sex should not be considered a sign of excessive vitality and capacity for sexual enjoyment. It may indicate an impoverishment of the personality, an impairment of the capacity to live a full, creative life and to relate oneself meaningfully to others as a whole person.

Qualitative variations of sexual behavior also are an expression of the total relationship which the individual has to himself, to the partner and to the role of sex. This refers as much to the preference of certain positions in the sexual act as to the so-called "sexual perversions." To explain sadistic or masochistic patterns on instinctivistic grounds is not a psychological interpretation of biological phenomena. It is the biologization of psychological phenomena. It prevents the real understanding of their dynamics. Only by uncovering the meaning of the so-called perversions with regard to their interpersonal and intrapsychic functions can the way be opened to effective therapy.

No isolated sexual phenomenon can be used as a criterion of emotional health or neurosis. Some analysts regard achievement of orgasm as a decisive criterion of progress in the analysis of female patients. While this may hold true for some patients in whom anxiety, self-rejection, hostility or the fear of losing control has prevented orgasm, it is wrong to consider the occurrence of orgasm always a criterion of emotional health. Orgasm may occur in connection with the satisfaction of severely vindictive, self-effacing or narcissistic needs, and in neurotic-symbiotic relationships.

The holistic approach sheds new light on two further phenomena: the role of sex in dreams, and in the emotional experience of severely detached patients. The frequency of sexual symbols in dreams has been considered proof that sexuality dominates the unconscious emotions of the dreamer. While dream interpretation soon learned to differentiate between manifest and latent content of the dream, sexual symbols remained, as it were, exempt; they were regarded as expressions of sex as such. But the dream uses the entire realm of animate beings and inanimate matter to present the dreamer's total feelings and to dramatize his conflicts. Viewed holistically, the language of sex (including such symbols as castration, or acquisition of a penis, or varieties of sexual behavior) appears as a highly expressive code to denote the great diversity of our *total* interpersonal relationships, our conflicts and our attempts at solution.[3]

A similar re-evaluation is needed with regard to the meaning of sexual images in the associations and fantasies of severely detached patients. The *total* experience of an interpersonal relationship, being beyond the scope of perceptions of such an individual, becomes so limited that sex alone is left as an essential symbol of human closeness.

THE INTERPERSONAL ASPECT

The role of sex cannot be correctly evaluated as long as the love and sex relationship is seen in a mechanistic way as a shifting of sexual energy from a Subject A to Object B. However, this view is at the bottom of the orthodox analytic concept of love and sex. The act of loving is seen as a transfer of libido from one person to another. "Being in love," says Freud, "is a state suggestive of a neurotic compulsion which is traceable to an impoverishment of the ego in respect of libido in favor of the love object." The result is that the lover loses, the loved one gains. In Freud's words: "Love in itself, in the form of longing and deprivation, lowers the self-regard, whereas to be loved, to have love returned, and to possess the beloved object, exalts it again." [4] Freud here describes an important phenomenon which involves the relation between love and self-regard. But, as often, he takes a neurotic process as representative of a general, healthy relationship. He deals neither with healthy self-regard nor with healthy love. To him, self-regard is a combination of "childish narcissism, omnipotence, as experience corroborates, and gratification of object libido." The concept of healthy self-regard based on the genuine acceptance of a strong, real self is foreign to him. And that state of "being in love," which he correctly calls a neurotic compulsion, really is the state of "neurotic love" which we observe in patients whose intrapsychic equilibrium is severely disturbed, so that their self-regard depends entirely upon getting love. Nor does loving mean losing for the healthy individual. Healthy love gives as much, or even more, to the lover as to the loved one.

When Freud speaks of a "love object" or "sex object," his description is pertinent to a psychological phenomenon which really exists. This, however, is not typical of an emotionally healthy love or sex relationship, but of the way in which the neurotic is driven to use—misuse—the love or sex partner as an object in the service of his own neurotic needs. The terms "love object" and "sex object" impress us correctly as indicative of a "de-humanization" of love and sex.

Sex, which in a healthy relationship can be the expression of love, here becomes the carrier of neurotic needs; needs for getting affection and approval, sadistic trends to dominate or live vicariously through the partner, search for glory through conquest, attenuation of self-contempt through the feeling of being loved.

The neurotic does not move spontaneously toward the partner. He is driven, without being able to direct or control the drive. As an unsaturated chemical compound is always ready to absorb the missing oxygen molecule from the environment wherever it can find it, thus, compulsively and unspecifically, the neurotic is driven to affection and approval, or triumph through conquest. He will take them wherever he can get them.

The partner, expected to function as the object for this satisfaction, is liked and "loved" if, and as long as, he or she fulfills this function, but becomes disliked or hated as soon as the function ceases. What is specific is the neurotic drive only. The partner is not experienced as a specific person. He is exchangeable and often exchanged.

The fulfillment of this neurotic function by no means depends exclusively, or even mainly, upon the actual personality or behavior of the partner. For example, the partner of the person who is filled with feelings of self-rejection and self-contempt automatically loses in value at the very moment when she accepts him. And the partner of the aggressive, conquering type exerts even less influence on the relationship; it is not he, as a person, who fulfills the neurotic need, but the act of conquest itself. When the conquest is accomplished, much or all of the attraction, frequently labeled "love" by the patient, will vanish.

Thus the dilemma of the neurotic is great. He cannot love but he needs to be loved. He cannot choose because he is driven. But, which is worse, he cannot *see* people as they are. Walled off as he is from others, in the fortress of his defense structure which has only small, thick, safety-glass windows through which to look out into the hostile world, the neurotic's perception of others is severely impaired. It is distorted by his own irrational fears and needs. He sees others almost as he sees the inkblots on the Rorschach cards. His picture of the other person is determined by his own needs, wishes, magical expectations and externalizations.

The psychological mechanism by which the picture of the potential or real partner becomes far different from reality operates to some degree in almost any love relationship, but most strongly in so-called "romantic" love. Stendhal calls this process *crystallization* and describes it as follows:

> After twenty-four hours of exposure to love, this is what happens in the lover's mind: if you throw a branch shorn of its leaves by winter into a deserted pit in the Salzburg salt mines, when you recover it two or three months later you will find it covered with brilliant crystallizations. *The original branch is no longer recognizable.* What I call crystallization is the operation of the mind that draws, from everything it is confronted with, the discovery that the loved one has new perfections. . . .

Crystallization may temporarily enrich the lovers. From the analytical viewpoint it is a source of unavoidable dilemma because the closeness of everyday reality is apt to dissolve these crystallizations. Their color reflects the color of the neurotic's needs. He endows the partner with just those qualities he most needs to find.

A self-effacing patient, with extremely strong dependency needs, endowed his wife with the qualities of a generous, warm, maternally loving woman. Occasionally surprised by the absence of any evidence of such love, he explained it as her inability to express emotion. However, this was nothing but an externalization of one of his own main characteristics. Well protected by this crystallization, his wife deceived him with several other men.

Dependent persons with strong wishes to be free from the responsibility for their own lives endow their partners with a magic capacity for caring, understanding, and guaranteeing security. They panic when more and more of these crystallizations crack under the impact of real events. The role of sex itself is completely overshadowed by the elemental force of their compulsive needs. Their intensity often is experienced as a state of sexual infatuation or as an insatiable hunger for sex gratification.

The self-effacing girl, alienated from her real self, is driven by extreme need for affection, for being liked, for "belonging" to someone. She cannot say "no." She is afraid to lose another person by refusing a sexual demand, whether or not she really likes the patrner. Asked, later, about her sexual experience, she will often say, "Oh, I did not mind it," thereby clearly indicating that her sexual experience did not serve as enjoyment, but constituted a payment for the satisfaction of her dependency needs— a payment which she expected to raise her self-esteem. But it did not and it could not do so. To such a person, sex may look like an almost miraculous way out of self-doubt and self-contempt. But the sex experience itself becomes quickly devaluated. "Oh," she says to herself and, not too rarely, to the partner, "he wants me only for *that* and not for myself." More and more claims are made on the partner, who has to show that he "really loves her." The insatiable need of the self-contemptuous person who is convinced that she is unlovable is certain to destroy the relationship.

The predominantly aggressive, expansive person puts sex in the service of self-glorification. To a man of this type sex becomes a battlefield, a testing ground for the establishment of his "masculinity." He records each conquest much as the fighter pilots used to make a mark on their planes for each enemy machine they had shot down.

The person whose neurotic pride is invested in conquest

often needs resistance in the partner. Without it, the relationship quickly loses its value for him. He derives a special thrill from crushing the partner's emotional resistance. A patient said, "I knew that the moral principle of the girl was against her doing it, but just that motivated me to get her. It gave me a tremendous feeling of power." The aggressive person often is completely unconcerned about the partner, ignores her feelings. He stands on "his rights."

Sometimes a man who is driven by his need for self-glorification *appears* interested in the fact that the female partner reaches her orgasm. But the way in which he is interested in it is more reminiscent of one who, at a fair, tests his strength by swinging a mallet onto a lever which shoots up to ring a bell, while his girl friend watches. He feels personally offended if the bell fails to ring. His neurotic pride, invested in his potency, is hurt.

This is not a rare phenomenon. It will be repeated in any relationship as long as sex functions as a weapon in the service of self-glorification. The relative frequency of this phenomenon does not, however, justify the prescription given in a recently published sex manual: "To keep peace in the family, the frigid woman might even be advised to pretend to have an orgasm. This would flatter the average husband and tend to keep him at home."

Sex information is by no means identical with sex education. The neurotic often uses "facts" in the service of vindictive-sadistic needs and for the externalization of his conflicts. Kinsey's statistics about the average duration and frequency of the sex act and about the symptomatology of orgasm were misinterpreted as a "norm" which *should* be reached. Failure to reach it often intensified self-contempt or led to its externalization onto the partner. Men became enraged when some of the described symptoms of orgasm were lacking; and a female patient with repressed competitive, sadistic needs began to check the "masculinity" of her husband in terms of minutes and seconds.

To the predominantly detached person sex often becomes inordinately important as a substitute for real human closeness, as the only available bridge leading out of his ivory tower. But his oversensitivity to what he experiences as coercion makes him irritated, frightened, even enraged, when he feels that he is expected really to share emotional experiences, or to commit himself to a relationship. Such a person may want and enjoy sex if *he* initiates it. But he may become furious when the partner wants it or when he feels that it is expected of him. He soon gets a feeling of being used. To comply with the wish of the partner is, he feels, a defeat, a surrender of freedom.

Sex is then tolerable only as long as it remains impersonal. The major part of his love and sex life takes place in his imagination. The partner of such a person might well ask, even during physical contact, "With whom is he deceiving me now?" Asked for that real human closeness which is part of a healthy sex relationship, the detached person often responds with anxiety or rage, expressed sometimes only in psychosomatic symptoms, sometimes by real panic.

THE INTRAPSYCHIC ASPECT

A healthy love and sex relationship requires genuine acceptance of the self as much as full acceptance of the partner. Only the person who truly accepts himself is able to accept the partner as an individual in her own right. The closer we are to our real selves, the better able are we to give love and sex the quality of a constructive experience. At the same time it becomes more likely that love and sex experiences will contribute to our emotional growth.

A few words are indicated here about love as a curative force. It cannot be doubted that to receive love and affection is a helpful—and often vital—experience, especially for a person who grew up in an atmosphere of emotional starvation. But what another person does for a neurotic cannot undo what he does to himself—for example, hating or trying to destroy his real self. In the self-effacing as well as in the vindictive individual, love may perpetuate the existing neurotic pattern. Only when the inner conflict becomes solved and the energies which were bound in the neurotic structure are set free can love—will love—contribute to emotional growth.

The neurotic structure draws energy away from the center, the real self, in a centrifugal direction to feed the idealized image and to fortify the compulsive defense mechanisms at the periphery.[5] Genuine self-acceptance includes the acceptance of one's own body and one's natural sexual role. Early alienation from the real self, especially when it reaches the degree of strong, unconscious self-rejection, creates the soil in which doubts grow about one's true identity, acceptability, lovability and about one's sexual role. I believe that the origin of homosexuality is closely related to an extremely severe, early alienation from the real self and a strong, destructive rejection of it.

A highly important expression of unconscious self-rejection is its externalization in the form of a negative body image. This may involve the whole body, its size, shape, smell, or any special part of it, from the color and type of the hair, shape of nose and ears, to the measurements of the waistline, the width of the hips, the curve of the legs and size of the feet. The negative body image centers with particular frequency in the breasts of the woman and the penis in the man. Culturally fostered stereotyped concepts of masculinity and femininity reinforce the significance of the body image.

The negative body image plays an important role as an externalization of the feeling of being unlovable. To deprive the patient of this externalization, for example, by means of a nose, breast or skin operation, without analytic therapy—which, incidentally, very often removes the need for the operation—is apt to produce highly negative results. In many cases it leads to depression, aggravation of the neurosis, self-destructive attempts or psychotic episodes.

The phenomenon of the negative body image as an externalization of hostility against, or rejection of, the partner often constitutes the basis of what is wrongly called "physical incompatibility." One of its expressions may be complaints about size and shape of the genital organs.

One important manifestation of alienation from the real self is the feeling of emotional deadness. Such a person craves love and sex like a blood transfusion, a vitalizer which provides, for moments at least, the feeling of being alive. Like the statue in Rilke's poem he asks:

> *Will no one love me?*
> *I shall be set free from the stone*
> *If someone drowns for me in the sea,*
> *I shall have life, life of my own . . .*

But if the statue comes alive, so the poem continues, it will suffer and long again for the sacrifice which has given life to it. In the same way, the person who is emotionally dead will yearn again and again for the vitalizing effect of being loved and stirred up sexually.

This is the tragedy in the neurotic's love problem. His capacity for loving is very small, his need to be loved tremendous. Alienation from the self and rejection of the real self exist, to some degree, in all neurotics. But with regard to love and sex a paradoxical situation arises: the greater this alienation and self-rejection, the greater the need to live vicariously through a partner. This explains the occurrence of the neurotic symbiosis.

An example of early alienation and self-rejection which predestine the individual to a neurotic symbiosis may be found in the character of Philip in Somerset Maugham's *Of Human Bondage*. Philip has lost both parents when a small boy, has been raised in a strict, loveless foster home and humiliated by his fellow students because of his clubfoot. He feels worthless, unlovable, has nothing but contempt for himself. But his alienation from his real self goes a step further: he actively rejects himself, rejects his own identity.

> He would imagine that he was some boy whom he had a particular fancy for. He would throw his soul, as it were, into the other's body, talk with his voice and laugh with his heart . . . . it was so vivid that he seemed for a moment to be *no longer himself*. In this way he enjoyed many intervals of fantastic happiness.

These intervals of "fantastic happiness" are achieved by means of the successful rejection of the hated self. He gets temporary relief from his self-contempt, but this active destruction of his own identity represents the strongest degree of self-alienation. Thus undermined he is bound to become the helpless victim in the morbid dependency relationship with Mildred, a sadistic, vindictive character.

The basis for a neurotic symbiosis may be provided by the satisfaction of any neurotic need. But I believe that two types of emotional dynamics in particular, separate or together, generate the energy for its enormously strong coherence: the dependency symbiosis and the magic mirror symbiosis.

In the former, neurotic needs for approval, affection, protection, "belonging," and avoidance of responsibility in the self-effacing partner meet the complementary needs of the expansive partner for aggression, domination, control, and the power to mold the other to his will. The expansive or sadistic partner in such a symbiosis often appears in the guise of a highly civilized husband or wife, a benevolent educator or generous sponsor who, like Professor Higgins in Shaw's *Pygmalion,* tries to raise the backward partner to his or her own high moral or cultural standards. This type of symbiosis temporarily provides a neurotic equilibrium in which the lack of assertiveness in one partner is compensated for by the aggressiveness of the other. But competitiveness, resentment and suspicion are only dormant.

Here the analysis of one partner may also effect constructive changes in the other. However, it is advisable for *both* to go into therapy. Otherwise the existing neurotic equilibrium may become disturbed without the establishment of a new, healthy relationship. If only the expansive partner is being analyzed, the self-effacing partner may experience anxiety because he begins to miss the aggressive and domineering qualities of his mate, which he experienced and needed as supporting strength. Or, if he harbors perfectionist trends, he may start to miss the strict standards of the sadistic dictator that were needed as a substitute for the values and the ability to take responsibility which he, himself, lacked. If only the self-effacing partner is being analyzed, his increasing assertiveness may produce friction and enrage the other, who may feel at a loss to understand why his victim no longer gratefully accepts his "generous education."

In the magic mirror symbiosis each partner supports the other mainly by functioning as a mirror of the other's idealized image. The partner is needed for protection against self-hate and self-contempt. Love and sex are used as a kind of alkalizer, to neutralize the acid of self-contempt which is being formed incessantly. This type of symbiosis indicates a higher degree of neurotic self-alienation and is therefore often found in homosexual relationships.

The idealized image of the expansive partner in this case includes strength, mastery and uniqueness; that of the self-effacing partner often contains—in addition to "goodness" and the ability to surrender himself in love—attractiveness, especially sexual attractiveness, which frequently will be experienced by this person as the main asset he has to offer. The self-effacing partner often unconsciously hopes to acquire, through a kind of osmosis, the desirable qualities of the partner, especially those which to him signify strength, independence, or, in homosexual relations, "masculinity."

This type of symbiosis is likely to break up at the very moment when the mirror mechanism ceases to operate. Strong, competitive hostility, always close to the surface, breaks through and the accumulated self-contempt and self-hate, no longer neutralized, lead to severe anxiety, depression, or self-destructive impulses. It is usually at exactly this time that such a patient enters the analyst's office.

The symbiosis remains a neurotic phenomenon regardless of which sex supplies the expansive-vindictive partner and which the self-effacing one. But it is characteristic of our culture that it accepts and even glorifies the dependency symbiosis if the expansive partner is the male, the self-effacing one the female. The aggressive, domineering he-man is glorified as truly masculine, even if he shows strong sadistic trends, as pictured in the movies by Humphrey Bogart. The submissive, compliant woman is often glorified as truly feminine, even if she is self-effacing to the degree of self-elimination. However, if the roles of the sexes in the symbiosis are reversed, the cultural evaluation changes completely. The variants of the expansive female and, especially, of the self-effacing male meet with severe condemnation. This intensifies the dilemma of the self-effacing male. His conflict is basically caused by the fact that his strong neurotic needs usually require *both* to be fully accepted and loved in the dependency symbiosis, and to have the means for self-glorification provided by the magic mirror symbiosis. But the simultaneous satisfaction of these needs is impossible to achieve. The symbiosis, by its very nature, leads to a severe exacerbation of his conflict. The self-effacing man, who fears rejection and longs for total acceptance, frequently harbors an idealized image of "purity" which may lead to paralyzing inhibition in sex. Therefore he chooses—or rather, as we said earlier, is driven to—the woman who is willing to take the initiative and the responsibility for the relationship notwithstanding his inhibitions. He welcomes the aggressive woman. Her attitude changes his experience of the sexual act from one of active assertion, which he still fears, into one of total acceptance which enables him to participate in the relationship and to function sexually.

Gradually, however, he begins to resent in the woman just those qualities which attracted him originally. Her assertiveness now is experienced as a tendency to dominate. To maintain the relationship, he also needs the support of his idealized image of being attractive, lovable and admirable as a man. However, this idealized image will inevitably become undermined as, in the process of everyday living, he becomes increasingly aware of his own dependency and passivity. Such awareness may be symbolized, for example, in a dream in which he gives his penis to his wife. The mirror function is bound to cease. His self-contempt, no longer neutralized, leads to depressions, listlessness, decrease and eventually disappearance of sexual desire, and even actual impotency.

The goal of analytical therapy in the treatment of these severely alienated patients, female as well as male, is the gradual overcoming of the destructive forces of self-hate, self-contempt and self-rejection, the mobilization of the constructive forces which lead to self-realization. Through solution of their deep inner conflicts, they become freed from the need for self-idealization and vicarious living and able to live emotionally by their own strength. Based on this strengthening of their real selves, they acquire the capacity to form a mature love and sex relationship.

The neurotic symbiosis, while it is often mistaken for "great love" by the partners and in literature, represents the extreme opposite from the analytical viewpoint. The neurotic symbiosis is a compulsive bondage of two weak, undermined selves who are chained together and support each other's neurotic structures. Thus the symbiosis maintains the status quo of self-alienation and prevents healthy growth and autonomy. Mature love is the voluntary sharing of two full lives, which enriches both partners and contributes to the growth and self-realization of both.

REFERENCES

1. Freud, S., *An Autobiographical Study,* Hogarth Press, London, 1935.
2. Horney, K., *The Neurotic Personality of Our Time,* W. W. Norton & Co., New York, 1937.
3. Weiss, F. A., "Constructive Forces in Dreams," *The American Journal of Psychoanalysis,* IX, 1, 30.
4. Freud, S., "On Narcissism," *Collected Papers,* IV, Hogarth Press, London, 1946.
5. Weiss, F. A., "Neurotic Conflict and Physical Symptoms," *The American Journal of Psychoanalysis,* VI, 1, 35.

Neurotic Guilt and Healthy Moral Judgment

MURIEL IVIMEY

That severe and intractable guilt feelings can operate as a serious block to progress in analytic therapy is well known by experienced psychoanalysts. One would assume that a sense of wrong doing would open the way to reorientation of values, constructive efforts, and realistic strivings toward healthier ways of life, but experience shows that we must reckon with a sense of wrong doing which is not only totally unproductive, but which tends to drive the patient toward chronic and unremitting self-torture, despair, and sometimes self-destruction. If this kind of guilt has been accurately understood and if the problems associated with it have been well analyzed and worked through, we find that the patient comes to experience a sense of wrong doing which has a totally different quality. There is no plunge into a hell of gloom and self-recrimination, but a sense of relief, of cleanness, a sustained facing of the issues, and the beginning of real hope and interest in remedying matters. We must conclude that

Read before the Association for the Advancement of Psychoanalysis at the New York Academy of Medicine, Jan. 26, 1949. Reprinted from *The American Journal of Psychoanalysis*, IX, 1, 1949.

we have to deal with two kinds of guilt feelings—one unproductive, obstructive, and potentially or actually destructive; and the other potentially productive and constructive. The title of this paper indicates this differentiation—neurotic guilt and healthy moral judgment.

A careful and serious study of Horney's theory of neurosis helps to clarify the serious technical difficulties encountered in dealing with problems of neurotic guilt and also points to the value of observing and utilizing the patient's true and constructive moral judgment. According to Horney's theory, neurotic or destructive guilt feelings are the outcome of neurotic developments. Neurosis inevitably entails impairment of moral integrity. This is expressed in a variety of ways. In some individuals, there is an intense conscious concern with moral problems, with right and wrong. But when we study the individual's moral values in detail, we encounter many glaring distortions and paradoxes. What is really bad has become good, and what is really good in human affairs has become depreciated and rejected. In other individuals, we see that the concern with what is good or bad has become such a confusing, torturing, and fruitless preoccupation that attempts are made to throw it out of consideration altogether, as a means to attain some peace of mind—only to have it recur with renewed intensity under the stress of inner tensions and external vicissitudes of living. In still other individuals, moral considerations have been successfully dismissed from consciousness, and the individual tries to get along in complete cynicism—leading to greater disturbances in the inner life and in relationships with others. The neurotic has, to a greater or lesser extent, become unable to distinguish or estimate what is realistically right or wrong, good or bad, in his attitudes, his thinking, and feeling about himself and about others.

By right or good, we mean what is good for a human being's personal growth, his development, and the fulfillment of his destiny as a whole, productive, and creative human being—untrammeled by neurotic inhibitions, uninfluenced by compulsive needs and undistorted by illusions about himself and others. When moral values are in harmony with what is good and right for human development, a person has a genuine appreciation of himself and others; he is guided by an honest and realistic appraisal of himself and others, and he is free to experience his own real, spontaneous feelings, to make the most of his real capacities and to explore and experiment with his potentialities. This would conduce to a full sense of living, to freedom in his relations with others, to spontaneous and active sharing with others, spontaneous and active contributions to the welfare and happiness of himself and others. Where there are irreconcilable issues between his own wishes and interests and those of others, he would be able to make a stand and come to a clear decision one way or the other and to take the responsibility for good or ill. As he grows in mental and moral stature, he could change his stand and his course of action, according to a better understanding of what is good for himself and others.

None of us knows finally what is good; we are prone to more or less imperfect moral concepts, but we can strive to clarify and then to reclarify them for ourselves and aim ultimately to cultivate them in their highest and best form. Our work as analysts entails helping others to solve their life problems. We do not determine for others what is good, but we seek to help our patients to free themselves from confusion and distortions so that they may determine what is good for themselves and direct their lives along the lines of their own spontaneous choice. It is inevitable that the analyst will indicate his own position through the very raising of questions, through indicating that there are moral issues at stake of which the patient has been unaware, through implications and sometimes through direct expression of his own personal opinion. But this is done in the spirit of stimulating free discussion and consideration of differences, where they exist. It offers the opportunity for each one, patient and analyst, to reflect, to reconsider, and to change if either one sees fit spontaneously to do so. Regarding what is good, I should like it understood that I am referring to basic, fundamental human values and not to conventional standards as set forth by special social, religious, or political ideologies. These standards may correspond to what is fundamentally good, or they may not.

As to a theoretical understanding of disturbances in moral integrity in neurosis, we would start with certain considerations upon which Horney focused in a series of lectures.[1] In them Horney concentrated on the split in the personality which results from the individual's attempt to create an illusion of wholeness when his personality is actually torn by inner conflicts which would otherwise exhaust and overwhelm him. The person tries to escape from his conflicts by letting his imagination construct a conception of himself in which there is or ought to be nothing at all the matter. In this conception all his contradictory traits, all his inconsistent thoughts and feelings, his whole neurotic way of life—all are entirely admirable and virtuous. He feels there is nothing really inconsistent or out of order about him. Since in imagination the sky is the limit, he goes further: the natural qualities and capacities he possesses become enhanced and transmuted into unique, superlative gifts; and still further, he can endow himself with capacities he simply does not have at all. This is the construction of the idealized image. But an illusion—no matter how necessary, or comforting, or relieving, or fascinating—is still an illusion. It does not erase reality. The fact remains that all is not well. The person is still bound to his compulsiveness and beset by fears, still suffers from inhibitions, weaknesses, and frustrations. He really has just average intelligence, or only superior intelligence; if he has special gifts they are probably undeveloped, and it would remain to be seen whether or not they are of genius caliber.

With idealization of the personality, the self as it really is becomes by comparison something to be ashamed of—unattractive, unworthy, a part of the personality which is always threatening to emerge and disgrace the person. It is his skeleton in the closet, or, as Horney has said, a disreputable poor relation who discredits and belies the image. We believe that this idealization of the personality is the direct cause-and-effect explanation of the individual's rejection of his real problems, his real abilities and limitations—and of his abysmal shame and guilt about them.

This development leads to a reversal of real human values. His inner life in a mess, the individual is so ashamed and disgusted he turns his back on himself and loses interest or faith in any capacity he might have to help himself. This is bad for him, but he feels it right and proper to desert and despise himself. His factual abilities fall so far short of what he can dream up about himself that he gives up the attempt to exercise and cultivate what he has. This is also bad for him, but he feels it good to be outraged at qualities and performance which fall short of a fantastic standard of perfection. This makes him, in his own eyes—and he thinks in the eyes of others—a superior person who detests "mediocrity," who knows what's what. But all the while he is not even trying to do what he can with what he has and from that point improve and become better. He hates others who are active and productive, and he feels good if he can spot their limitations and short-comings. This is again bad for him because it frightens him away from making any efforts of his own. Or he regards other active and productive people as specially endowed, favored by the gods, on a different plane. They have been allowed to "graduate"; they sit among the elite; what they produce flows out of them with no effort on their part. This is bad for him, for he has lost a sense of common ground with others. His thoughts eliminate the factor of effort which active people make to do or achieve something and which he also would have to make in order to be productive.

On innumerable finer points, the false and the spurious are given positive value. Being helpless, being inert, having nothing to do with others, pushing others around, bullying, overriding, being vindictive, paying others back, hating someone till one's dying day—these qualities can be elevated to the highest virtue, to a point of honor. And there are innumerable qualities related to what is really good which the neurotic repudiates as unimportant, unnecessary, not worth-while. The idealized image has seduced the conscience into accepting and approving that which degrades and stultifies, and into rejecting and despising attributes and capacities which would promote and stimulate growth and well-being. A person cannot get rid of neurotic guilt so long as the conscience is thus perverted. This perversion of moral values constitutes one of the crucial problems in therapy. This theoretical understanding enables us to clarify moral issues and to help our patients to achieve substantial gains in working out their problems.

I think it will help to clarify what I have just said if I describe briefly where psychoanalysis stood on the topic of guilt feelings prior to our recent advances. Freud saw his patients bogging down in irrational guilt feelings; he saw them sticking in a state of utter inability to break through, to dissipate guilt feelings and make progress in treatment. He saw that these persistent and chronic, tormenting self-accusations (on the score of sexual matters) were reactions to failure to conform to an impossibly strict and harsh moral code. He saw this code emanating from a hypothetical structure which he called the superego, and hypothesized further that this superego was addressing itself with blame and censure to the weak, impotent ego, or self, or I. He considered that the function of the superego was to regulate the drives of the primitive, completely amoral, instinct-driven id, or unconscious, in man. Thus the ego was caught between the superego and the id. Freud regarded severe, irrational guilt feelings and self-punishing tendencies as expressions of a force inimical to well-being, since the ego was unable to escape from or combat them, as evidenced by the bogging down in self-condemnation. He identified this force with a death instinct inherent in all animate matter, including man, which drives a person to destruction under pressures of guilt, or at least blocks the road to recovery and well-being. The forces of the id he identified with the life instinct, or pleasure principle, or Eros, which bids man to pursue happiness and fulfillment with no moral or ethical considerations.

How did Freud envisage a possible solution or salvation for the weak ego, caught between these two forces? He credited the ego with capacities to think and reason, but not with a capacity to grapple with moral problems, release itself from irrational self-accusations, or to establish sound moral principles and be guided autonomously by them. The patient must resolve irrational guilt feelings by rational repudiation of the dictates of the superego. He should be able to do this if he has understood and accepted analytic interpretations. But if he was successful in throwing off the yoke of the superego and freeing himself from irrational guilt, it was obviously impossible to permit the forces of the amoral id to have full sway in civilized society. Again, rationally, the patient must bring himself to accept the rational morality of society. This left the patient still subject to *instinctive* forces driving him in the opposite direction, and he would have to rely, theoretically, on the presumably less powerful dictates of reason. This problem —how the forces of life and death ultimately become dissolved or coalesced—was unanswered, as Freud states in the paper "Analysis Terminable and Interminable." [2]

Freud's attitude toward the part that guilt played in preventing recovery led to the conclusion that an inner sense of guilt was abnormal and undesirable. And this would seem to lead to the conclusion that Freudian analysis rejects morality. These factors have caused psychoanalysis to be viewed with alarm and indignation by many people. But Freud was a sincere and ardent moralist. He considered it essential that the patient give up the strangulating morality that precipitated a degree of guilt, that forced him into black despair and paralyzed his interest in life and efforts to get well. This is a point that many non-scientific students of psychoanalysis have not grasped. Freud considered it essential that the patient come to terms with unbridled exercise of primitive instinct, and he considered it essential that he reconcile himself un-equivocally with commonly accepted and necessary de-cencies in human society. This is a second point which some of his critics either overlook or of which they are not aware. Freudian psychoanalysis does and does not reject morality. It rejects the scientific study of problems relating to morality in neurosis, *and* it wants to help the patient solve them. The dilemma is solved by directing the patient toward external solutions.

THE RELIGIOUS VIEW OF GUILT

Since some religious leaders have crusaded against psy-choanalysis as being, in their opinion, an evil influence, I want to make a few comments on the two points of view regarding the role and value of guilt. Orthodox religion holds that it is an essential force in impelling the sinner to seek salvation and thus gain everlasting life. Freud, the scientist, sought to understand certain forms of human suffering and their alleviation and cure. Irrational guilt feelings were seen to obstruct recovery, a block to attain-ing peace of mind and freedom from conflicts and their devastating consequences. But civilized man must attempt to conform to the moral values of society. The doctrine of original sin in orthodox religion and the doctrine, ac-cording to orthodox psychoanalysis, that man is funda-mentally amoral, at bottom a creature of instincts—these two doctrines bear a close resemblance to one another. One, derived from Scripture, adheres to the account of the fall of Adam; the other is derived from a mechanistic evolutionary theory which holds that there are only quantitative differentiations in the development of higher forms of animal life from lower forms of life. According to this view, no qualitatively different and new factors appear in higher forms of life, such as, in man, a conscience or a capacity for moral judgment. From an orthodox religious point of view, salvation from a state of sin and from punishment in the hereafter is achieved through a sense of guilt, the acknowledgment of sin, the mystical experience of grace, forgiveness conferred by a minister of the church, and the acceptance of the moral teachings of the Savior. Man is credited with a capacity to appreciate and respond to morality emanating from a supernatural source, but not with a capacity to guide himself morally. From the orthodox psychoanalytic point of view, liberation from psychic suffering is achieved through insights and working through the problems thus revealed. Man rights himself through awareness and acknowledgment of his instinctual drives and the acceptance of good and decent social patterns. He has the capacity to appreciate and accept the guidance of civilized moral values but not to formulate a moral philosophy for himself and live by it in a responsible way.

A BROADER VIEW OF GUILT

We have seen irrational guilt feelings in much the same light that Freud did. They are one of the blocks in the road to recovery, and they must be dispelled. We have seen that they are expressions of a sense of failure to live up to impossibly high and strict standards of conduct and performance. But irrational guilt feelings have been studied in a much broader and deeper way and in much greater detail. The consideration of guilt feelings is not limited to those concerning sexuality, but it has been extended to include a sense of wrong-thinking, wrong-feeling, wrong-doing in all other aspects of a person's life. As to detail, we pay attention to the many ways in which guilt is felt and expressed—tendencies to scold oneself excessively, to accuse, berate, belittle and condemn oneself on account of real shortcomings and also on account of traits and behavior that are not in any way reprehensible. Related to guilt also are many vulnerabilities, fears of being found out, expectation of the condemnation of others, penalties and punishments which the individual inflicts on himself and on others. We also include manifestations of attempts to escape from self-accusations and self-contempt, wherein a person turns to condemnation and blame of others, suspicions of evil in others, seeking to make others feel ashamed and guilty.

The superstructure, or idealized image, whence come irrational self-accusations and guilt feelings, has been studied in more detail. This superstructure corresponds to Freud's superego but is radically different in concept. We would see it as a neurotic development, not as a universal instinctual manifestation; we would see it affecting all phases of the individual's life, not merely the regulator of instincts so powerful as to be uncontrollable by moral considerations. The idealized image is the creation of the individual's own imagination, called into being by the dire necessity to quell the chaos of his inner neurotic conflicts, so that he may function with some sort of equilibrium. The idealized image for each individual varies from that evolved in other individuals according to the particular neurotic character structure. We would not envisage a universal "superego" which approves and disapproves the same thoughts, feelings and behavior. According to our concepts, what one person would hold valuable and would feel ashamed and guilty about would be unique for him, and such things could be quite different from what another person would obsessively strive for as an ideal and obsessively despise himself for failing to recognize.

We have considered the irrational nature of neurotic guilt feelings, and we have seen that they represent one of the impairments of moral integrity resulting from neurotic developments. We might say that the factor in human nature subserving moral judgment—that is, conscience—is thrown out of gear, over-activated, supercharged, inflamed by the nagging complaints of the idealized image, or overwhelmed and paralyzed because of sheer inability to satisfy the impossible demands of the idealized image. Conscience cannot function according to true values; a person is at the mercy of a conscience which misdirects him. It approves and sets up as good much that is actually bad and it fails to register what is wrong with the real self and to point out a right course.

Freud's concept of ego was never very clear, probably because he ignored qualitatively new factors in human nature, especially the new and highly sensitive and highly discriminating factor of conscience as part of human personality. Our concept of self, corresponding to the nebulous Freudian ego, is that it is the vital core of personality containing potentialities for personal growth, development, and fulfillment. In neurosis these constructive forces, including moral judgment, have been to a large extent diverted into the service of safety requirements—first against an actually adverse environment in childhood; then into over-charged, anxiety-driven compulsiveness; then into defenses against inwardly generated anxieties caused by inner conflicts; then into false solutions of conflicts. With the construction of the idealized image, one of the false solutions, the individual turns against his real self and irrational, neurotic guilt comes into play. What is "good" for the patient is strictly determined by his inner necessities for safety and equilibrium. He becomes, of necessity, totally one-sided and must keep himself blind to connections between his distorted values and the many serious disadvantages and the suffering that are thus incurred. The greatest of his sufferings is neurotic guilt resulting from his turning against himself.

THERAPY AND GUILT

We would tackle problems of neurotic self-accusations and irrational guilt feelings as follows: since the individual has made up his own idealized image (which bids him despise himself) he can unmake it, provided he comes to a genuine appreciation of the extent to which he has abandoned himself to his imagination and of the mischief thus created. Irrational guilt feelings are not the expression of a self-destructive, or death, instinct, but the reaction of the real self which is tyrannized and beaten down by the individual's imagination of what he ought to be. When the patient dispels his illusions about himself, irrational self-accusations and self-frustrations cease. This can be a long and arduous process, but it gradually opens the way to a reorganization of values and considerations of what the patient spontaneously wants to do about his life.

The first job at hand is the question of the person's own treatment of himself as a human being. His attention is called to self-deception, stultifying pretenses, how he has made up a story about himself out of whole cloth, how he has entered into a self-perpetrated plot to cheat and abuse himself. The reduction of the idealized image and of irrational charges against oneself is accomplished not entirely by rational processes, not entirely as a result of logical explanations, not as a result of reassurances from the analyst that he really is a worth-while person, but as much and more by calling upon the patient's moral judgment, however weakened and warped it may be. We would see to it that such questions as the following emerge in the course of the work of analysis: Is this right, fair, just, honest that a person so deceive himself, that he so shame and stigmatize himself? And for what? For weakness, for being in trouble, for being afraid, for being confused, for having lost his way, for having only the good resources he does have and not the supreme intellectual powers or the goodness of a saint—even for having resorted to foul play against himself and others in his desperate attempts to keep going on any basis? What is he doing to himself with this great overblown, fantastic notion of himself and with this brutally self-recriminatory attitude toward himself which crushes all his confidence and self-esteem?

The products of a conscience inflamed by the idealized image are irrational guilt feelings. The products of a conscience relieved of the overload of impossible demands are normal, productive guilt feelings concerning personal shortcomings and weaknesses that actually ought to be set right and can be set right. With productive moral judgment there comes a sense of hope and anticipated achievement if one is genuinely and wholeheartedly in process of working at one's problems, and a sense of peace and well-being with each success. A clear distinction is to be made between neurotic and healthy guilt feelings. Neurotic guilt obstructs progress; healthy guilt provides effective leverage to go forward and make changes. Neurotic guilt causes constant and endless pain if it is experienced directly. If it is not experienced, the neurotic individual has avoided it by resort to some anesthetizing device, which brings suffering anyway. Healthy guilt feelings are associated with pain, but of a quality which is immeasurably less poignant because of the sense of wanting and being able to change.

This distinction is essential in the dynamics of therapy. If the therapist does not make the distinction and thinks only of guilt feelings in general, he is bound to make one of two mistakes:

1. Coming upon irrational guilt feelings, he might recognize them correctly as obstructive and problematic, arising from too great demands the patient makes upon himself. But he might stick to this attitude toward any guilt feelings and fail to recognize constructive moral judgment which would serve as a stimulus and directive for the patient in working at some problem. He might unwisely minimize or soft-pedal healthy guilt at a time when constructive moral judgment needs confirmation and encouragement.

2. If the therapist's attitude is that guilt feelings in general should stimulate the patient to work, he may be hasty and superficial toward tormenting neurotic guilt feelings and overlook problems related to the idealized image which need to be worked at. This attitude could wreak unnecessary hardship and suffering for the patient who is still under the tyranny of an idealized image and not yet on sufficiently good terms with his real self to be interested in himself.

MORAL VALUES

Where guilt is not experienced consciously, where it is invisible, where it is cloaked in symptoms or appears only in occasional outbursts, I believe the problem is best approached through a consideration of the patient's moral values. In the earlier years of our psychoanalytic practice we are constantly startled by the chaotic state of the patient's values and dismayed by the apparent absence of any values at all. If one focuses on this scrambled morality, one will find in every analytic hour many expressions of distorted values. Whether or not we take them up for discussion immediately is subject to considerations concerning selection and timing of interpretations—but it is essential that distorted values be noted and discussed at some time. Tentative comments are sometimes quite fruitful and often lead to fuller and more specific revelations in this area. If the time is ripe for questioning the patient's values—and I am all for free experimentation but not reckless attacks—the sooner the patient becomes aware of the disorder in this area, the better, and the sooner constructive moral judgment is awakened.

The distinction between neurotic self-recrimination and irrational guilt on the one hand and positive, morally critical attitudes on the other is readily made if one observes the patient's reaction to some discussion of moral issues. In the first case, irrational guilt feelings would be accompanied by depression, fatigue, hopelessness, inertia —the characteristic bogging down; or by anxiety concerning coming to the next analytic hour; or resentment against the analyst, accusations that the analyst is trying to make the patient feel bad or a complaint that the analyst is not supposed to inject anything relating to moral judgment into the analysis. Such reactions are signals pointing to attempts to ward off the pain associated with neurotic guilt. Very strong and persistent resistance to the topic of moral values is a warning to proceed cautiously or to postpone until the patient is stronger. For irrational guilt is related to self-hatred and has a self-destructive component.

On the other hand, constructive moral judgment on the part of the patient, expressed in a realistic appraisal of some characteristic, is experienced with some pain—but there is, along with pain, a feeling of interest, wanting to stay with an issue, to re-examine it as if in anticipation of something hopeful and profitable to be done about it. One feels a sort of inner concentration in the patient, and his productions are more in the nature of his wanting to reflect on his own, rather than appealing to the analyst's judgment or arguing a point with him. If the analyst recognizes this in the patient, it is important to leave the patient to his own reflections unless invited to participate. Remember, too, it is an invitation to participate and not to take over. Many points will come up between analyst and patient on which there is plenty of room for genuine and honest differences of opinion. In case of such differences, the issue for each will be based on what is essentially right and wrong, and each will feel he can genuinely respect the position of the other. Many other issues will be cloudy to the patient, and he may wish or need some help in direction—direction in the sense of orientation, but not management or dictation. Under these circumstances it is the analyst's responsibility to offer personal opinion if it is timely according to the patient's readiness to appreciate it as a personal opinion.

The recognition and utilization of constructive moral judgment are two of the most important contributions to our present practice in therapeutic analysis. Freud seems only to have considered non-productive, irrational guilt feelings and not to have recognized the constructive potentialities of spontaneous, healthy moral judgment in human nature. His concept of constructive forces in the therapeutic process was limited to the patient's rational faculties and what was called positive transference in his relations with the analyst. We would say that irrational guilt feelings are the products of an overburdened conscience, that conscience is a natural and essential part of human nature. When relieved of the excessive demands of the idealized image, this "organ" of moral judgment operates as a sensitive gauge to indicate inwardly for each individual what is really good and what is really bad, what is right and what is wrong.

REFERENCES

1. Horney, K., "The Search for Inner Unity," lectures delivered at The New School for Social Research, Spring 1949.
2. Freud, S., "Analysis Terminable and Interminable," *Int. J. Psychoan.* XVIII, 1937.

A Psychoanalytic Understanding of Suicide

ELIZABETH KILPATRICK

As we look about us, we are struck by the tremendous tenacity with which all living things hold to life, and the tremendous intensity with which they struggle toward creative growth. Yet, in spite of this life force, some human beings destroy themselves.

The suicidal act is one outcome of the decisions: "I will no longer put up with myself as I am," and "I will no longer tolerate this world as it is." These decisions occur to many human beings at one time or another. The healthy person utilizes them as an incentive for making constructive changes in himself and in his environment. Others destructively shape the environment by creating an imaginary world into which they retreat. Others destroy fellow human beings whom they believe make life impossible for them. Only a few destroy themselves.

Read before the Association for the Advancement of Psychoanalysis at the New York Academy of Medicine on March 24, 1948. Reprinted from *The American Journal of Psychoanalysis,* VIII, 1, 1948.

HISTORICAL VIEW OF SUICIDE

We are impressed by the widely varying attitudes which have existed, and still exist, toward suicide. Even among primitive people there is no uniformity. In some tribes suicide is unknown, in others it is common. Some tribes regard it as despicable, and others as the only fitting answer to a trifling insult.

Among civilized people at one time or place, suicide has been regarded as contemptible. In England, for example, it was regarded as a crime; and the body of the victim was submitted to all sorts of indignities, while his property was confiscated by the state. In India the practice of *suttee*, in which the widow burned herself on her husband's funeral pyre, became a praiseworthy sacrifice approved by the state. In Japan, persons were encouraged by the state to expiate a crime and avoid humiliation by *hara kiri*—an honorable suicide.

It is of interest that these practices are no longer approved. Our cultural pattern places value on the individual's assuming responsibility for his behavior and the consequences of it. In both primitive and civilized society, the incidence of suicide varies with the value placed on the individual as a human being. Where there is no striving for leadership and prestige, suicide rarely occurs. Where ambition and rivalry are keen and unity weak, it is frequent.

Religions have all taken definite stands against suicide. Yet in all ages and in all sects, some individuals have confused self-sacrifice with self-destruction, by making the suffering the major goal in the sacrifice. The sufferings voluntarily endured by many of the early saints were the equivalents of suicide, and bear a striking similarity to acts we see in neurotic people today.

The lowest suicide rate has been in Roman Catholic countries and among Roman Catholics in any community. Certain characteristics of this denomination point, then, to deterrents against suicide. Among these may be included: the authoritarian attitude against suicide, the threat of punishment, the relief of guilt feelings through the confessional, opportunities for atonement of sins committed, and the unity of the church.

In all countries at all times the suicide rate is low when economic, political, and religious standards are high, but it increases as they decline.

From this brief survey, we would conclude that external factors—which include moral and religious standards, economic conditions, and cultural patterns—do serve as stimulants or deterrents to suicide. It has always been recognized, however, that personal dissatisfaction with life has been the important deciding factor. Newspapers tell us one middle-aged man commits suicide because he has an incurable disease, another because his usefulness to his community is at an end, and still another because he has gone bankrupt. A schoolboy ends his life after failing in an examination. A woman commits suicide after her husband's death, and another because she could not do her job well.

We are struck by the fact that each of these reasons given is a condition to which some other people adjust satisfactorily, continuing to live and make constructive use of their available potentialities.

SECURITY OR PSEUDO-SECURITY

Let us contrast the characteristics of the individual who is able to accept the exigencies of life with those of the individual who feels overwhelmed by insurmountable difficulties. The former has a strong incentive for living and for creative growth. He has self-confidence. He appreciates the qualities of other human beings, and avails himself of their knowledge and experience. He assumes responsibility for himself and for the consequences of his behavior. He can move wholeheartedly into situations. When external circumstances alter his way of life, he can form new relations. Such an individual will have no wish to injure himself. Life is full of possibilities to the end.

The neurotic person, on the other hand, feels that this is a hostile world. To him the most important thing in life is to be safe. All his resources are devoted to this purpose. His adaptations to the world continually choke off his potentialities. He is dependent on others for an evaluation of his ability and a knowledge of his rights. His attitude toward himself and others varies with the success of his safety devices. His observations, judgments, and values are subjectively determined. Such an individual, predominantly anxious, tense and beaten, to whom every new situation is a threat, will easily relinquish his hold on life.

PSYCHIATRIC VIEW OF SUICIDE

Those psychiatrists who are not psychoanalytically oriented have not been aware of the inner motivating factors in the suicidal individual. But they have made helpful clinical observations. They have observed that suicidal patients have deep feelings of guilt and self-accusation. Such patients are not in good rapport with any other human beings and are secretly vindictive. Suicide may be attempted at any time, but particularly when the patient begins to improve. A person who has once attempted suicide will repeat the attempt each time he becomes ill.

Psychoanalysis has stimulated thinking in the direction of unconscious motivation and inner conflicts. Freud's hypothesis that each individual has a life instinct with impulses toward creativeness, and a death instinct with impulses toward destructiveness, pointed to inner conflicts as an innate characteristic of every human being. Several psychoanalysts have published their results of the application of Freud's theory of neurosis to the problem of suicide. In *Man Against Himself* Karl Menninger states, "Both destructive and constructive tendencies are originally self-directed, but become increasingly extroverted in connection with birth, growth, and life experiences. . . . When there is a forcible interruption in these external investments, or when too great difficulty is encountered in maintaining them, the destructive and constructive impulses revert back—upon the self. . . . If defusion occurs, the destructive tendencies lead and may permanently prevail so that self-destruction supervenes."

Horney's theory of neurosis sets us thinking in new directions. Some of her concepts relating to this problem are: there are constructive tendencies in man toward spontaneous creative growth. When untoward environmental factors in early life threaten individual security, anxiety develops. This is counteracted by patterns of behavior which are safe in that particular environment and in consequence give the individual a feeling of superiority. These behavior patterns become neurotic trends and, being unconscious, motivate compulsive behavior which inhibits constructive development. The function of neurotic trends necessitates the development of many which are incompatible and result in inner conflicts. These further impair healthy growth and generate anxiety. As a result the neurotic character structure is being continually reinforced by new unconscious defences. Each step in this kind of development further alienates the individual from his healthy self. He loses his normal self-esteem and the ability to evaluate himself as a person. When he feels safe in the environment, he has spurious feelings of pride and superiority. At other times he feels anxious, inferior, and contemptuous of himself.

Our contention is that self-destructive tendencies are not innate, but the consequence of accumulated self-contempt. The neurotic individual's security is continually threatened by contradictory trends within himself and lack of verification of his superiority from the outside. Neurotic pride is replaced by self-contempt, and there is a constant intrapsychic struggle to restore it. This struggle is reflected in attitudes toward self, interpersonal relations, and productivity.

An important part of the neurotic structure are unconscious solutions whose function is to maintain inner unity by keeping neurotic pride in the ascendancy. The most significant neurotic solutions in neurosis with suicidal impulses are detachment, living in imagination, externalization, and the idealized image. Detachment and living in imagination eliminate awareness of any failure of superiority by pushing reality into the background. Externalization permits the individual to live his psychic life through others. The idealized image attempts to replace the real self by an imaginary perfect self. When these solutions are neurotically successful the individual feels he is a superior being. He is arrogant and withdrawn emotionally. He becomes increasingly alienated from himself and others and is increasingly unable to cope with reality. This adds to his anxiety and contempt for himself. He retreats more and more into his neurotic solutions. The nature of neurotic development is such that the untreated neurosis becomes more severe and self-contempt accumulates. The patient makes unconscious efforts to tolerate life by retreat from reality, and by various forms of destruction to self and to others.

A CASE OF SELF-DESTRUCTIVENESS

Martha, basically insecure as a result of early oppressive interpersonal relations, attempted to allay her anxiety by complying with all the demands of her prestige-driven parents. She could always be depended on to give up her own interests without complaint and to outshine other children by model behavior. Later her compliance extended to all her interpersonal relationships.

This type of growth cut her off from spontaneous development and from acquaintance with her real potentialities. That she did battle to some extent for her rights as a human being was indicated by anxiety attacks in the form of night terrors, bed wetting, stomach aches, and unexplained temperatures from time to time. But this rebellion is already that of a withdrawn, self-destructive nature, and contrasts with the aggressive temper-tantrum behavior commonly seen in children.

Detachment was a prominent trend. Early she acquired the habit of running away from home, and later she would isolate herself for hours and read and fantasy. In imagination she was the little princess who suffered but was always kind and forgiving. Gradually her behavior became predominantly compulsive. Her detachment and compliant trends conflicted with one another and with repressed aggressive trends. For example, she was driven to be alone, but her compulsive need for approval forced her to seek companionship. She must excel in everything, but all achievement had to appear effortless. It became increasingly difficult to satisfy these contradictory drives. She felt anxious and angry but was unable to express her fears except through tears and suffering.

The most satisfactory relief from anxiety was physical illness; in time even this failed to be successful. She also attempted to bring about inner peace by synchronizing conflicting trends in an idealized image. In this image she incorporated all the qualities she thought superior in a human being and derived tremendous pride from seeming to have reached it. As a result of this device, she was further alienated from herself and from reality.

Martha saw herself as superior in terms of difference and uniqueness. She would excel but would never be in competition. She saw herself not detached, but admired for her dignified reserve. She felt she was "good"—as defined in terms of giving service. This in turn verified her lovable qualities, and assured her being given the best of everything without asserting herself. She considered her intellect was such that she would be admired for the ease with which she could accomplish any task, and her psychosomatic illnesses spared her from being envied by others. When she believed herself to be her idealized image, she felt grandiose in her superiority. But everyday living, achievement in work, and interpersonal relations continually threatened this belief. At such times she drove herself relentlessly to restore her belief in her imaginary self. Sometimes she was so worn out with struggling that she accepted illness with deep gratitude and often fantasied death. At times she believed herself to be the opposite of her idealized image and was sunk in self-contempt and despair. Then endless solutions were tried to restore her pride. Each attempt led her deeper into self-destruction. For example, she had surreptitious relations with men of low moral standards which temporarily restored her pride and then plunged her into self-contempt. She blamed all her failure and distress on others and thereby lost friends. She created situations which brought illness and suffering to herself.

This way of living had the consequences of destroying all the constructive forces in her life and gradually took her farther and farther from her real self. She resorted to drugs in a half-hearted suicidal attempt.

When a neurosis follows a course similar to this, there seems to be no choice but suicide as a terminal solution. My experience has been that cases of neurosis which terminate in suicide have many of the characteristics seen here. I call attention particularly to the nature of the neurotic solutions, the alienation from self, and the cumulative self-contempt and hopelessness.

In such cases the individuals are forced to function in response to the unconscious demands of an idealized image so exacting that it can rarely be satisfied. They are constantly driven by *musts* and *shoulds* and have a prevailing feeling of not living up to something which is essential in life. This results in a consistent attitude of disappointment, dissatisfaction, and belittlement of themselves. Being alienated from themselves, the worth of these individuals as human beings depends on other people's opinions of their achievement. Since their trends are predominantly detachment and compliance, they must keep close to people in order to be of service and be reassured. They must keep a distance from them to be admired for their perfection. They must be outstanding but must never compete. These unrealistic contradictory demands force them to make excessive claims on others. When these claims are not met, they are fearful and hostile. This hostility is never expressed openly. It is repressed, transformed into self-hate, or expressed in subtle surreptitious ways such as vindictive triumph or sadism.

Another reason for self-contempt is that their performance falls consistently below the average. This is the result of a tenuous relation with persons and things. Nothing seems of value and they do not enter wholeheartedly into any undertaking. They try to restore neurotic pride in many ways. They withdraw from other people, they cultivate the attitude that they are all right and that all their difficulties are due to external circumstances. They live extensively in imagination where they are gentle, sensitive, and misunderstood. They triumph vindictively over others through fantasies of humiliating them or making them feel ashamed.

The solutions for self-contempt are invariably nihilistic in character, and as such are gradually destructive to the person as a whole. These people run away from problems, either leaving them to someone else or not recognizing they exist. They experience feelings of unreality. They resort to drugs, alcohol, psychosomatic disorders and, finally, suicide.

THE NEUROTIC VALUE OF SUICIDE

Suicide as an escape from self-contempt differs from the other nihilistic solutions in that it serves the additional function of restoring neurotic pride. I shall demonstrate, by clinical material, that in the suicidal act there are two objectives: to get rid of the hated self, and to restore pride. It is significant that although the solutions resorted to for relief of self-contempt are nihilistic, the greatest fear of these patients is of being annihilated. The suicidal patient expresses fear of: becoming less than nothing, being blotted out, losing identity. One recovered patient said, "The phrase 'only a splash on the wall' kept repeating itself." The danger which threatens seems to them to come from the outside, but on analysis we find them terrified by their own self-hate and hostility.

The suicidal decision is a victory of a kind over this worse fate that they believe is without. A patient said recently: "I dreamed continually of going down in bottomless pits. I feared becoming inhuman, an outcast in the world. Death was known. It happened to everyone. To die would mean to be like other people." In this case the suicide would be a means of maintaining her identity.

While accepting suicide as one of the nihilistic solutions for dealing with self-hate, my contention is that the decision will not be made unless there are deep hopelessness and alienation from self. And, most important, it will not be carried through unless the act affords an opportunity for restoring self-pride.

The relief from self-contempt and the restoration of pride may be accomplished through the suicidal act in such various ways that the cases seem to divide themselves into groups.

HOPELESSNESS LEADS TO SUICIDE

One group includes those in whom there is a well-developed neurosis. Relations with other people have become strained and hostile. Attempts have been made to maintain pride through neurotic love, living in imagination and vindictive triumph. Self-hate has been constantly gaining in ascendancy. Everything seems hopeless, and the resources within the self less and less. The act of suicide is the final event in this cumulative struggle and has two objectives of equal value: to destroy oneself and to make the other suffer.

The story of Anna Karenina in Tolstoy's novel is an excellent example of such a case. Anna was beautiful, charming and graceful, but had no appreciation of her real value. As we become acquainted with her, we learn she has a tremendous pride invested in subjecting others to her charm; and when she fails to do this, she is anxious, depressed, and irritated with herself. As time goes on, the unfriendly attitude toward herself increases to contempt. She attempts to restore her pride in various ways which are ultimately destructive to herself and to others. Her insatiable demands cause her to feel constantly mistreated. She has not the slightest regard for the dignity or welfare of any human being. Her interpersonal relationships deteriorate into means for vindictive triumph. She strikes out wildly in every direction for her rights and refuses anything offered her. The chief target for her externalized self-hate and her hostility is her lover. She is constantly driven to an attitude of antagonism. She says, "He loves me, I know—he asks for tenderness, but some strange force within me will not let me surrender." She describes a feeling as of some evil spirit of strife she could not exorcise from her heart.

In this world of hers, half reality and half fantasy, she stumbled on an idea—and all at once she was at peace. She knew it was an idea that solved all: "Yes, to die—the shame and disgrace of my husband and child, my awful shame will be solved by death. To die! And he will feel remorse, will be sorry, will love me, will suffer on my account." She would obliterate self-contempt in death and retrieve her pride through making the other suffer. She was aware of her own inner struggle. "I will escape from everyone and from myself."

In situations where there is less opportunity for vindictive triumph, the danger of suicide is less. For example, a patient with a tremendous self-contempt which he attempted to diminish through love told me frequently of his impulses to jump from his fourteenth story window. He asked once: "Will you tell me how you would feel?" As I considered my answer carefully, he added: "I am afraid I know. You would shrug your shoulders and say: 'I wish I could have been of more help to him.'" His interpretation of my response to his question failed to reinforce the suicidal impulse.

ALIENATION LEADS TO SUICIDE

In a second group of cases, death is not the major purpose of the suicidal act. I have in mind the neurotic person who establishes inner peace by unconsciously erecting an idealized image and its opposite, a despised image. His major problem, then, is to ward off anxiety and self-contempt by keeping the two images separated. This becomes increasingly difficult as the neurosis becomes more severe.

Oscar Wilde describes, in symbolic form, this type of conflict in *The Portrait of Dorian Gray*. You recall that narcissistic young man who experiments with endless solutions to maintain his youth and beauty—this being his idealized image. The main solution attempted is to separate from his physical self all undesirable features. This is accomplished symbolically by attaching them to a self-portrait—his despised image. He is reassured, yet terrified, when he sees how ugly the portrait is becoming. The attempts at separating himself from it become increasingly devastating to his personality. He is being overwhelmed by self-hate. He makes one desperate effort to be free by killing the despised self—the portrait—but it is part of him and he dies—accidentally.

A neurotic person may transfer all his self-hate and anxiety to one particular part of his body. He then feels well except for the pain in, or appearance of, that part. He attempts to change it or to get rid of it. If he takes things in his own hands, the procedure may result in death, or in mutilation. He may seek the aid of physicians and often succeeds in having operations. These either fail or only temporarily relieve the anxiety since the organ removed was only a symbol of the real problem.

One patient complained constantly of "something rotten" in her abdomen. When physical examinations failed to disclose an abnormality and she was not given the surgery she demanded, she tried to relieve the condition by opening her abdomen. When hospitalized, without being given psychotherapy, she became increasingly anxious, and after many threats finally committed suicide.

In all of these cases self-hate is concentrated on the whole or part of the physical body, and attempts are made to bring about inner peace by attaining bodily perfection. Death may be an accidental result of their own efforts to get rid of the part they believe affected. Or, being unable to get rid of the imperfection, they feel hopeless, and avoid what they think a worse death by attempting suicide.

The drive for perfection may take the form of achieving some unusual physical accomplishment. Then the need for self-glorification is so great that life is not taken into consideration. I have in mind cases similar to the rejected lover who wrote, "My death will be so wonderful I will be admired by you." I would include here also many persons who are driven to daredevil acts to accomplish something never done before.

One of my patients was noticed floundering in the water and losing out against the tide. He refused the help offered, but fortunately recovered in time, and shouted, "You might as well give me a hand here." This man had such an inflated idealized image of himself that he could not conceive of failing at anything. He supported this thesis by almost complete unawareness of the world about him.

In some cases with similar character structure, the perfection sought is in abstract qualities, and the same technique is used to maintain it. If, for example, the intellect fails to verify the idealized image, they cease to use the intellect and seek perfection in other qualities. In persons of this suicidal group, the perfection demanded is concerned with the physical self, perfection of appearance or ability; and the whole or part is destroyed as it fails this function. These patients, detached and narcissistic, seemingly in love with themselves, have presented a baffling problem for the therapist. When we understand narcissism not as love of the self but as love of the idealized image of self, we become aware of the amount of self-hate and alienation which must be present. Our emphasis in therapy then focuses on uncovering and analyzing all of the implications of unconscious pride and self-hate, with gratifying results.

SUFFERING LEADS TO SUICIDE

Other neurotic individuals who resort to suicide have exaggerated emotional attitudes toward suffering. Some will not tolerate suffering—it is beneath their image of themselves to suffer—and others find a positive value in it. Such attitudes can be demonstrated by individual reactions to chronic physical disease. One such invalid continues to use what potentialities he has to make life meaningful; another holds tenaciously to life as though to do that in the face of such suffering were a virtue in itself; another commits suicide. In this suicidal solution, the act symbolizes a victory, it affords an escape from a worse fate which he knows will overtake him. There are many suicides in this category at the beginning of a psychotic episode.

The manic depressive patient having a similar fear attempts suicide towards the end or at the beginning of a depression. He may be able to verbalize his feelings, and says, "I am terrified of another attack." The fears are always related to being destroyed as a person—becoming less than nothing. This is the anxiety many patients feel throughout a depression if they make the slightest move. They try to avoid it by giving up entirely to self-contempt, and living a vegetative existence. In time there is a change —a step nearer reality and conflict becomes active again and with it more ability to do something. When the sufferer decides on suicide, he brings about the very thing he has feared may happen—annihilation. But having made the decision himself, there is definite relief. He avoids the humiliation of destruction by destroying himself, and thus attempts to restore neurotic pride.

When suffering of itself is of value, it may take the form of a suicidal obsession. Each time, when faced with a slight failure, the thought comes: "I must kill myself." Each time when about to make productive effort, the thought comes: "If this does not turn out well, I *will* kill myself."

This tentative solution temporarily relieves facing the consequence of failure, but time is spent in contemplating ways and means and consequences of suicide, with the result that only a minimum effort is put into the work at hand—and the only satisfaction, if the work is completed, is that it is completed. This results in a general decrease in the quality of the work done, and a very real reason for dissatisfaction or even contempt of self. Life for these individuals contains one failure after another in educational, economic, and personal relationships. Consequently there is very real suffering. Suicide may seem to be the only solution and yet there is hesitation.

The main trends of another type of patient are detachment and compliance. Such a person values self-sacrifice, service, and goodness very highly, and uses other people as opportunities to satisfy these needs. When the suffering takes the form of physical illness, there are many neurotic values. Illness gives the patient an opportunity to detach himself, and to rest, as well as an excuse for failure and its consequences. It brings demonstrations of love in the form of gifts and visitors, and verifies his uniqueness in being able to be cheerful even though handicapped. The suffering, although detrimental to constructive growth, may prevent suicide. One patient, in discussing the length to which suffering could go, said, "I can get arthritis and be a complete cripple. Then I would be so ugly I would commit suicide."

Psychosomatic illnesses may replace or alternate with suicidal impulses as a means of avoiding self-contempt. One patient came to analysis in a panic in relation to fear of being inducted into the army, and at the same time fear that he might be rejected. The former would mean subjugation to the will of another, exposure of his inability to do everything better than anyone else, whereas rejection would mean he was not as good as the others. Suicide was the only solution. When this man began analysis, his suicidal impulses quickly faded out of the picture, but ill health became a very prominent factor. There were frequent colds with fever which developed into chronic coughs, frequent gastro-intestinal disturbances, skin rashes, etc. He worried about these, consulted many doctors, but had difficulty in following medical instructions. He was able to talk about his excessive demands on himself and how well he felt when everything went well; but how, with the slightest failure, he developed a physical illness which occupied all his attention. When he was finally able to face his self-contempt, suicidal impulses again came into the picture and alternated with psychosomatic complaints as the first reaction to each new problem.

Both of these solutions act as retarding forces in analysis by making it impossible for the patient to put forth constructive effort. With the psychosomatic solution, the self-destruction goes on, but becomes the responsibility of fate or his physician toward whom he may become very vindictive. The suicidal solution, on the other hand, is his sole responsibility. In this case the suicidal solution was discarded early in analysis, indicating a dependency on the analyst. As he became stronger, he showed more variation in meeting problems, sometimes constructive effort, and sometimes destructive in the form of suicidal impulses or psychosomatic complaints.

MURDER AS VICARIOUS SUICIDE

I will briefly discuss murder as a vicarious suicide. The story of Medea demonstrates this dramatically. Medea was ordered to aid in the destruction of Jason, her father's enemy. But she fell in love with him; and, driven by her feelings, she not only saved him, but plotted against her father and brother to promote his interests. After years of devotion, she was rejected by Jason. She was consumed with self-hate and humiliation at having permitted herself to have loved him. She decides to kill herself, but hesitates. Out of her anguish comes the thought, "No, that is not the answer. They would make a holiday. He would not be sorry. He is responsible for my humiliation and he must suffer."

She is the slave of vindictive triumph. She discovers ways to make Jason suffer that include killing their children. But she loves her children and hesitates. They are a part of her. Yet she is driven to kill them. She ponders over their gentleness and tells herself, "If you do not kill them, they will die by the hand of foes." She kills them and, symbolically, she kills the part of her she hates—her own love and tenderness which brought on her humiliation.

One of my patients during a depression continually berated herself but did not make any suicidal attempts. She did, however, attempt to kill her two sons but not her daughter. She said the boys were morons like herself and she wished to spare them from all the suffering she had to endure. In time she recovered from the depression and lived comfortably apart from her husband but on friendly terms with him.

Seventeen years later when her husband decided on divorce, she had a second depression with suicidal impulses. During the course of analytic treatment, she became conscious of her self-hate with all its ramifications. We were impressed by the extent to which it had been consistently externalized to her husband. Under the guise of friendliness and cooperation she had continually tried to hurt him. The murder of their sons would have served the function of relieving some of her self-hate, which she had been vaguely aware of, and of vindictively triumphing over her husband, a need of which she had not been conscious. During the years she had lived apart from him, her self-hate had been kept in check by her success in vindictively triumphing over him. She had accomplished this by remaining married to him but living apart, and by keeping him separated from his children.

SUICIDAL PATIENT IN ANALYSIS

The analysis of a suicidal patient is conducted in the same way as any other analysis except for the precautions necessary on account of this special symptom. In all cases the factors leading up to suicide give us an indication of the values which are important in maintaining neurotic pride for that particular individual. This information will be helpful in therapy. For example, when a patient attempts suicide after the death of her husband, we know her to be a person lacking in self-assertion and to whom dependency is essential. We know that her husband played an important role in her ability to maintain neurotic pride. We know she has a great deal of deeply buried self-hate and hostility. Such an individual will require a great deal of support early in analysis.

During the course of every analysis, intepretations frequently induce self-contempt. When this occurrence is accompanied by suicidal impulses, more than usual care must be taken to graduate the interpretations in relation to the patient's growing strength. Thus we avoid an excess accumulation of self-contempt.

The analyst's attitude towards the patient is even more significant in these cases than in the average. Hopelessness and apprehension on the analyst's part concerning the suicidal patient is immediately felt by the patient. In analysis, as elsewhere, self-destructive individuals express aggression and hostility in the form of suffering and suicidal threats. The patient's dilemma may seem to indicate concentration of the self-destructiveness, but no improvement will take place unless the hostility which is invariably present is analyzed at the same time. Interpretations which emphasize self-pride or self-hate without following through on all the implications of each, and the relation of one to the other, will activate self-contempt and self-destructive impulses.

Suicidal impulses arising during analysis may be aroused by an event outside analysis which activates self-contempt. A patient became suicidal after the will of an uncle was read. He had left his money to another niece. "This was as it should have been," she reasoned, for her cousin was poor. Had he left it to her, she would have given the money to her cousin. The reason for her depression was that his will demonstrated to the world that he liked her cousin better than he liked her. This belief reinforced her low opinion of herself. Such occurrences during analysis open up new avenues to unconscious sources of neurotic pride.

Suicidal patients have tremendous self-hate which is partially released through externalization. Aggression is so repressed that early in analysis externalized hate may appear only in dreams and fantasies. When hostility can be expressed toward the analyst, there is a temporary relief from suicidal impulses. The hostility can then be further exposed, and cautious analysis leads to its source as one of the unconscious means of relieving self-hate. An analyst who is overly kind, severe, or detached may endanger the patient who has suicidal tendencies by making it difficult for him to express hostility.

CONCLUSIONS

Suicide occurs only in severely neurotic individuals.

It is one of the solutions to excesses of self-hate which may happen in every neurosis.

Solutions to self-hate in patients with suicidal impulses have the quality of insidious destructiveness to self and others.

Suicidal impulses occur in patients who feel self-contempt, hopelessness, and who are alienated from themselves.

Suicide is resorted to when there is overwhelming self-hate and when the act affords an opportunity for restoring pride.

Psychosomatic disorders may alternate with suicidal impulses in a self-destructive patient.

Various neurotic solutions which temporarily relieve self-hate will temporarily relieve suicidal impulses. These solutions include the externalization of self-hate to overt expression of hostility to others, living in imagination, and dependency on a partner.

During psychoanalysis insights which activate self-hate may arouse suicidal impulses. The danger of suicide, during treatment, will be diminished in direct ratio to the analyst's understanding of the neurotic process, his sensitivity to the patient's tolerance for insights, and his appreciation of the patient's necessity to take refuge at times in neurotic solutions which relieve self-hate.

Moral, religious, economic, and familial influences act as temporary deterrents to suicide. The only effectual cure for suicide is changing the neurotic character structure through psychoanalysis. The important changes achieved will be in the patient's inner relations with himself, the elimination of self-destructive tendencies, and the replacement of neurotic pride by healthy self-esteem.

Karen Horney on Psychoanalytic Technique

I. THE QUALITY OF THE ANALYST'S
ATTENTION · *Morton B. Cantor*

The analyst's attention includes understanding and the taking in of observations. This is to be differentiated from the passive receiving of impressions. For the analyst, attention is directing himself—mind and body— to the whole being of the patient, with the purposeful view toward action (therapy). It is not only the application of intellectual energy. We are focusing on getting a feeling for the patient, for his uniqueness, so that his differentness no longer feels strange to us. This is of fundamental importance. There are three aspects to the quality of the analyst's attention—whole-heartedness, comprehensiveness and productiveness.

WHOLE-HEARTEDNESS

The whole-hearted aspect of the analyst's attention involves observing with all one's capacities and faculties.

Compiled and edited by Dr. Cantor from lectures on psychoanalytic technique given by Karen Horney at the American Institute for Psychoanalysis during the years 1946, 1950 and 1952. Reprinted from *The American Journal of Psychoanalysis,* XIX, 1, 1959.

Here we are listening, seeing, and feeling with our intuition, undivided interest, reason, curiosity, and specialized knowledge. This knowledge involves awareness of our own selves, generalized professional knowledge and experience, and all that we are aware of in the particular patient. We are focusing ourselves as fully as we can on all the patient's communications, verbal and non-verbal.

Whole-heartedness is an ideal state, an approximation of one's own personal equation. It is the faculty of not being distracted, either by our own deeper problems or by situations which have upset us acutely. The mind is the analyst's tool, as is the equation of our total personality, and we have the obligation to keep this tool in good shape if we are to do such concentrated work with it.

As an example, Horney spoke of feeling herself yawning and being terribly tired while seeing a patient upon her return from a vacation. Doing some quick self-analysis, she thought of a letter she had received from an old friend reminiscing about the wonderful time they had enjoyed together. Horney became aware of the conflict between the recently completed life of full ease and the present return to concentration on other people. The patient had been talking about the movie, "Treasure Island." In it the cook who had been a compliant person became captain. It had been this which touched Horney's problem, namely, resuming responsibility. She felt alert again and the problem of tiredness was no longer disturbing.

Detached, alienated psychoanalysts who are living through their intellect may be good observers, acute listeners, and able to concentrate better because they are disturbed very little by their own feelings. They have an interest in their patient's problems, but are more interested in the structure of the person than in the human being.

Not only must one's intellect and stored-up knowledge come into play, but also one's emotions in regard to analytic work. It means laying oneself open for all the numerous feelings that can exist between two people—not only curiosity, but likes, dislikes, dismay, disappointments, humor, hopefulness, anger, sympathy, and so forth. This may be disturbing at first, but in time, as all remnants of feelings are allowed to enter, it will gradually become less irritating and more rational. The emotions of the analyst which will arise will be geared more to the patient than to himself; that the *patient* is getting somewhere, instead of the analyst getting him there, will be the central issue.

With greater awareness of the patient, we may finally approach the ideal of whole-heartedness—a surrender to the work by letting all our faculties operate while nearly forgetting about ourselves. Horney compared this to surrendering oneself to music or getting a first impression of a work of art. As our knowledge and experience become an integral part of ourselves, we are barely conscious of all that we are while at the same time *being* all that we are. We can then be freer to extend the boundaries of ourselves and be more open to the beings of others.

COMPREHENSIVENESS

After considering the analyst's availability and openness to himself and the patient, the next aspect of concern is the specific direction of our attention. In comprehensiveness, we strive for the ideal of taking in everything without focusing exclusively on a limited set of factors. Horney compared this to the driver of an automobile who has to be aware of the condition of his car, the roads, the weather, other cars. Gradually this concern becomes automatic, so that it doesn't interfere with effective functioning.

The equivalents in the analytic situation have been discussed in detail in the previous articles, "The Initial Interview" [1, 2] and "Interpretations." [3] In relation to the comprehensive aspect of attention, Horney re-emphasized observation of the patient's tempo in therapy and how it changes, and thinking in the tenor and spirit of the patient's associations. We are talking here about the many different levels of awareness the analyst can sense and observe.

Are we paying attention to the pauses, pressures, and rhythm of what is going on? What is the quality of the eagerness to learn something, the active searching for something? Eagerness may be deceptive; glib interpretations without interest in the analyst's opinion may arise from the patient's need to show how much he knows. Is the eagerness only intellectual or primarily an eagerness to confess? Does the patient give the result of his self-analysis or does he arrive at it during the hour, letting the analyst participate?

It is important to observe what is changing in the patient's attitude. Is he productive and is he now productive outside of the analytic hour, too? Is what he is saying pertinent, or is he floundering and scattering? Does he focus on the intrapsychic or the interpersonal features of his problems? Does he have a tendency to deal with concrete things or theoretical considerations? What is his reaction to what the analyst is saying?

On another level, how is the patient presenting himself? Is he merely complaining, feeling victimized, apologetic, or demanding? Does he talk about himself primarily in terms of others? Is he critical, grateful, over-grateful, on the defensive, or glorifying himself? Does he give very complex accounts? What does he omit? Does he talk with the aspect of doing as much as possible, or showing what he has learned?

In regard to feelings, does the patient only report them or does he experience them in the hour? The feeling of anger, relief, headaches, dizziness may often have a dramatic quality indicating that something is going on at an experiential level. Is there an attempt to look for deeper meaning to these feelings? Is the patient noting a sorry state of affairs, or really experiencing suffering?

With one patient who showed no outward manifestations of anxiety and had a desperate need not to experience it, the only way I could sense his anxiety was by the change in the tempo and spirit of the hour. Suddenly he would mention ten or fifteen different problems in passing and I felt myself getting slightly dizzy and breathless, as if I had been trying to catch a butterfly. It was only by paying attention to my own emerging feelings that I could get a picture of what was going on.

To approach the goal of comprehensiveness in our attention, we need to be flexible enough to take in all those various elements as they come up. Horney talked about listening idly, avoiding a pin-point concentration which can close us off from a truly holistic view of the patient. In this regard, she mentioned the definition of a learned person as one who has forgotten a great deal of detail because he can afford to put it aside. The learning process leads to learning more and experiencing more freely, with the focus on our own individual theoretical concepts *arising from* this. We must also be careful not to let the intensity of our attention convert a mutual analytic situation into one where the patient is in the brilliant spotlight on a clinical stage while we are in the darkened audience. With both of us sharing more subdued light in the same room, we can become more open and real to one another.

PRODUCTIVENESS

While we listen and observe, something comes to our minds and quite unconsciously a pattern may form. We may not always be sure what is going on, but it may come after an individual hour, the next day, or much later on, depending on our availability to ourselves and to the patient. Is what is going on in our attention to the analytic situation productive?

We talk of productiveness in the sense of starting something going. What is really changing and what has to be tackled further? Are trends and solutions less compulsive and feelings more alive? Is the patient more aware of understanding his own drives and desires? Is he more confident in the analyst, more independent, more accepting of responsibility? Are there fewer neurotic symptoms and fears of conflicts? Perhaps there are more physical symptoms in the patient who has heretofore not been close enough to his physical being to be aware of bodily participation in emotional conflict.

A woman began analysis with a vague feeling that something must be wrong. After two years she was still denying any deeper conflicts, resisting the concept that her dreams or slips of the tongue had any meaning; analysis seemed to be at a standstill. There was no evidence of psychosomatic symptomatology; nothing could be specifically pointed out to her that she could accept as an indication of anxiety. I confessed a concern about a "stalemate" in the analytic situation and said, "We'll have to light a fire under you if we're going to get anywhere." That night she developed her first psychosomatic symptom, a painful burning and itching around her anus. For the first time she began to seriously consider that there was a connection between physical and emotional processes, that there were unconscious forces operating within her, and that perhaps a person was something more than a rational human being operating behavioristically to overt aspects of his environment.

The ever-present question is: "Is what is going on now leading to self-awareness and bringing us closer to self-realization?" This applies on all levels—the doctor-patient relationship, the patient's life outside of the analysis, the description of an event or feeling, the discussion of a dream or interpretation, free-association, and what is going on within the analyst himself. How much can have happened with the patient in analysis if nothing happened to us while working with him? In a successful analysis, something happens to both people. If the analyst is merely a catalytic agent and nothing has changed in him, how much really could have gone on within the patient?

ATTITUDES INTERFERING WITH THE QUALITY OF ATTENTION

Many of the attitudes interfering with the analyst's attention have been discussed in "The Analyst's Personal Equation." [4] The analyst who is trying to get places in a hurry, rushing toward an understanding, will be impaired in terms of whole-heartedness, comprehensiveness, and productiveness. This may result from his own "shoulds," pride in omniscience and intolerance toward being confused, and from avoiding being in anxiety and conflict himself. His own egocentricity will interfere with his whole-heartedness. A one-sided view of what is going on within the patient may also be part of where the analyst is in terms of his own self-analysis (e.g., focusing on self-effacement and minimizing expansiveness).

Approaching the patient with preconceived ideas restricts comprehensiveness. Freud coined the term "free-floating attention," but for him much of this was an intellectual floating concerned with fitting what he observed clinically into the theories he was formulating. This may be done with anyone's own theoretical formulations. Here is the advantage to a theory with a general framework. The theory should never be more important than the patient. It should serve only as a blueprint. Of course, no one can be free of all one-sidedness, but from the point of theory as a background and with enlarging experience, the analyst can reach a more constructive balance.

IS ANALYSIS AN ART OR A SCIENCE?

Considering all the elements involved in the analyst's attention, the discussion led to whether analysis was an art or a science. Horney felt that people who say it is an art may wish to discredit analysis as merely a talent, something that someone is born with. Science can't tell you about *your* dog, but about dogs in general. This may help you, but to know *your* dog, you must live with him. In this sense, personal knowledge and understanding rather than generalities are considered art.

Analysis is more critique than criticism, an appraisal of all aspects of what is going on rather than a judgment *about* them. We are more concerned with the information communicated to us by the patient than with knowledge of the patient in an abstract sense. Analysis must not be purely "objective" to be scientific. It is scientific in the broad sense of seeking for what is, seeing patterns and cause-and-effect, having a method and an element of predicting future events. But it is also an art in the sense of creativity, freeing the way for a change of structure and helping to bring about that which is more harmonious with full living.

REFERENCES

1. Cantor, Morton B., *The American Journal of Psychoanalysis*, XVII, 1, 1957.
2. Cantor, Morton B., *The American Journal of Psychoanalysis*, XVII, 2, 1957.
3. Slater, Ralph, *The American Journal of Psychoanalysis*, XVI, 2, 1956.
4. Azorin, Louis A., *The American Journal of Psychoanalysis*, XVII, 1, 1957.

Karen Horney on Psychoanalytic Technique

II. UNDERSTANDING THE PATIENT AS THE BASIS OF
ALL TECHNIQUE · *Emy A. Metzger*

Analysis is a cooperative enterprise; the analytical situation is a process going on between two persons for the purpose of helping the partner who is sick. Yet though both partners have this common purpose, their ultimate goals differ. The patient's goal is divided: consciously he wants to understand himself, his compulsiveness, his fears; but he is unaware of his inner need to maintain the status quo, to actualize his neurotic fantasies, to live without limitations according to the dictates of his idealized image. He expects magic help and he demands it. The analyst's goal is undivided: he strives for truth, for an understanding of the patient and his difficulties, their development and their present manifestations. He sees the patient as he is today and is interested in this human being's growth and in those factors which have impeded healthy development. His focus is on the road toward self-realization and on those forces which obstruct this road. The analyst brings to this task his interest, his professional training, his expe-

Compiled and edited by Dr. Metzger from lectures on psychoanalytic technique given by Karen Horney at the American Institute for Psychoanalysis during the years 1946, 1950 and 1952. Reprinted from *The American Journal of Psychoanalysis*, XVI, 1, 1956.

rience, his feelings, his wish to understand. Yet he is an outsider from the start.

The patient is involved; he has the raw data, but is interested only in some of them and may even be driven to hide or distort vital parts of them. Living in fantasies, he is often unaware of this distortion of reality. When the analyst tries to understand the patient's difficulties this effort will help to interest the patient again in those aspects of himself which he may have eclipsed, effaced, overvalued or thwarted.

WHAT IS "UNDERSTANDING"?

Understanding is a social and specific human process, a moving with one aspect of our being toward the stand which another person maintains, but while so moving still maintaining our own stand. Therefore, we can never be completely where the other person stands—we stand *under* the person's stand; we understand his position, and it is this which enables us to compare his stand with ours. Human relatedness with the partner permits repeated moving back and forth between his and our own position. Each new move may reveal a new aspect of his personality structure and bring into focus deeper and deeper levels. However, such a process of interrelatedness is possible only if we accept and are tolerant of the partner's stand even if it does not coincide with our own. Our feelings of compassion help us to see more and more of the stand of the other. Understanding is therefore a movement of emotional and intellectual energies. If we lose our own stand altogether, we would not have understanding but blind surrender. If we stand by with a detached, purely intellec-

tual, reflecting evaluation of a person according to conventional "given" standards, we have a "mirror" attitude.
It would not be participation but would lead to a mechanical classification of the patient's personality according to
an established generalization, as for instance Freud's approach has manifested. However, real understanding is
a wholehearted and receptive observing and "feeling into"
the other person with all of one's own self. It leads to more
and more comprehension of an individual patient with his
individual personality and his individual problems.

UNDERSTANDING AT THE START AND DURING LATER PERIODS OF ANALYSIS

Knowledge of one's own self, which Socrates already has
thought important for healthy living, is a basic prerequi-
site for the analyst. In his own analysis he has become
aware of previously unconscious aspects of his own personality structure. This permits him to spot and recognize
trends and drives in the patient of which the anxiety-
ridden neurotic is unaware. Remembering his own need
to allay arising anxiety when, during his own analysis,
protective defenses were endangered, he will become aware
of the patient's blockages, his efforts to procrastinate, to
become elusive, evasive or to ward off premature insights.
He will register such strategic maneuvers, understand and
keep them in mind though the time may not be ripe and
the patient not yet ready to tackle them. Besides, the analyst may not yet have a clear enough understanding of their
significance in this specific neurotic structure.

The initial process of spotting single impressions can be
compared with the experience of being in a forest. There,

one may first see very little: general outlines, shades, colors. After being in the darkness for a while one may recognize here a tree stump, there a branch, some moss on the ground, a wilted flower. At first these impressions may be meaningless and disconnected, but gradually one may differentiate more, see here or there a familiar form, a connecting link. Walking on, a new turn may bring into focus other aspects which may now explain particulars heretofore un-understandable. Again the view may become obstructed and then may reappear, but from a different angle, when a new vista is reached. From such beginning awareness of seemingly disconnected factors, the process of analysis moves constantly toward many directions of understanding and comprehending. Rational and irrational forces can become clearer; the intensity of neurotic solutions may be appreciated. All these factors are interwoven, just as they are in a forest.

In analysis one may first become aware of the pervading influence of "pride" in a person's life. Later one recognizes specific prides and then their ramifications, connections, and growth-inhibiting qualities. Or, a general recognition of righteousness may lead to the spotting of militant righteousness in one person, to the recognition of a defensive righteousness in another. Needless to say, this growing understanding occurs also in the recognition of different "shoulds." At such a point we may ask ourselves, "What is this particular person doing to himself?" Or, if one finds *lebensneid*, "What is he begrudging?" Such questions may sharpen our senses toward further searching, recognizing and understanding.

Constantly, new problems arise. With each new problem the process of understanding moves from the general to the particular, then again from the particular to the general. Somebody may have a hostile attitude toward others. Then he may exhibit his self-hatred or, instead, he may be irresistibly driven into a feeling of being abused by others, or, he may be particularly frightened by insights. In another person whom one may have considered friendly and kind, one may suddenly spot callousness; later his need to depreciate others may become overt though it is deeply hidden under a surface attitude of admiration. In still a later hour, we may become aware of his tendency to begrudge those who, in one specific aspect, seem better off than he. There may be many conflicting manifestations, yet under closer study, they all stem from the same root. Let us take the patient who shuns pride: in another hour his craving for affection may become evident; later, he may reproach himself for certain unimportant matters. These first, apparently disconnected trends will finally fall together into the picture of the self-effacing personality.

In the constant back and forth, from the general to the particular and vice versa, these interrelations become more and more understandable and are recognized as belonging together. At a later point in analysis we may see how one such trend may lead to the next one; the whole sequence of neurotic solutions will become clear, as one factor connects with another one. Previously un-understood factors now appear embedded in this specific patient's personality structure. They are a link in the chain of neurotic development. Understanding the moving toward pride, we see how incompatible, conflicting drives may be the outcome of one and the same drive.

A good example of such contradictory manifestations of one and the same solution is self-effacement with the ultimate goal of dominating others by helplessness. The resulting pervasive, vindictive aspects surprise us at first, especially in a person who consciously believes herself to be saintly and good. When deeply hidden inner conflicts shape up more and more distinctly, we can feel their intricacies and experience their impact. At last the central conflict—health versus neurosis—will come into focus. By then we may have seen how the "inner logic of neurotic necessity" has led to a discarding of reality, to irrationality. We may have approximated the outlines of the "idealized image" which, unsubstantiated by facts, is as irrational as is the resulting pride with its satellites, the tyrannical "shoulds" and "self-hatred."

Understanding a patient will be incomplete if we do not become aware of the intensity of a person's specific neurotic forces and of his anxiety when feeling split open by individual inner conflicts. We then have to feel his neurotic and actual "real" suffering and experience the impact of his compulsive drivenness. Only when we ourselves understand the violence and intensity of all these destructive energies can we evaluate the patient's preparedness for entering the final battle, the struggle between the healthy and neurotic forces. Without such a "living through the intensity of the central conflict," the reality of this struggle cannot be fully experienced, as Rank and Ferenczi first recognized. It is like the difference between "being in jail" and "reading of being in jail."

THE ANALYST'S FEELINGS: HIS TOOLS

It goes without saying that understanding the patient becomes a function of our own relationship to ourselves. If we lay ourselves open without losing ourselves, we can listen wholeheartedly while simultaneously becoming aware of our own reactions to the patient and his problems. When, during an analytical hour we may feel unusually tired or bored we may re-examine the analytical situation and try to understand the meaning of our own reactions in relation to our own specific problems. Still-persisting remnants of our own neurotic solutions may have been stirred up by the patient's associations and by his acting out. Furthermore, we can evaluate the patient's conscious or unconscious technique of irritating us, of trying to distract us from the context, or of making a desperate non-verbal attempt to draw our attention to a specific aspect which previously may have escaped us. Without awareness of either participant, the patient may respond to the analyst's imperfections by vindictively exploiting them. By becoming alert to such stratagems we may understand their meanings. Our own inner self is an instrument which often can register such feelings and their meanings more quickly and more precisely than our intellect.

From the start we may have difficulties in understanding because we may over-focus on the content or be bewildered by a sudden turn which seems to confuse or contradict a heretofore logical sequence. But gradually, we can learn how to use our intuition, which is not a mystical quality but an understanding on a deeper level, and which observes more than we realize. While listening we may be tapping our great store of inner experience. Suddenly something may come up in our mind without our immediate awareness of why it comes up at this particular point. Horney recalled how a patient spent an hour talking with grief about the death of a relative. While listening, she recalled Ibsen's *Wild Duck* and the quotation, "In a year, her death will be for him a source of beautiful recitals." At this time the correctness of her associations could not be verified, but later they proved to be accurate. This patient had a personality structure similar to Ibsen's sentimental photographer who prostituted his own true feelings for propaganda purposes. He was equally self-destructive and helpless.

Needless to say our understanding does not limit itself to the patient's verbal communications. Every move, beginning with the first letter or phone call, every individual nuance in appearance, posture, clothing, tone of voice, or gesture may be experienced and understood in its significance for the patient's neurotic involvement. Changes in facial expression, moodswings, frequency of breathing, blushing and coughing may reveal important clues and awaken certain feelings, memories and associations. The degree to which we are interested or distracted may become a clue to our reactions to the patient's qualities, his moral fiber, his pain, his anxiety, his efforts to communicate. His attention to our interpretations and his reactions to them will become revealing if we are aware of our inner echo to his affect, or our lack of resonance to the impairment of his emotional energies. We may see superficial issues, complaints or repetitive themes dominating the foreground of his mind while associations more significant, yet vaguely experienced, are kept in the background. His more or less realistic or fantastic attitude toward vital problems may startle us at first, but later we may become understanding of his need to keep distance from them in spite of his urgent request for help. His need to perpetuate the status quo may become meaningful to us when we can understand how much energy he has spent in allaying anxiety, in erecting a façade, in avoiding a fight.

When all our senses have become familiar with his specific way of relating we may get a new understanding of his plight and of his need to keep its deeper meanings out of awareness. The better we ourselves become acquainted with this meaning the more will we be able to appreciate his inner suffering which may be dimmed by his compulsive needs to please, to impress, to retaliate. After we become attuned to the patient's individual ways of experiencing and relating, we will no longer think and interpret in technical terms but we will feel how to convey our interpretations tentatively. We will then interest him in the meaning of his associations by using his own language. Besides, we may be able to select whatever will be most important and most feasible to him for an interpretation of the material which he produced. Understanding his dilemma will make us tolerant of one patient's purely impersonal intellectual curiosity or another's need to confuse the issue or a third's attempt to show that he knows everything better. At other times we may tackle his specific ways of blocking his own progress. Such a difficult subject we will choose to bring up when we ourselves are relaxed and when the patient will be more resilient to such a hurt to his pride.

UNDERSTANDING CHANGES

Participating with all our faculties in the analytical process, we will become more astute about changes occurring in our patients, and in accounting for them. Knowing that symptomatic changes may have only limited value or may even reinforce pride in magical solutions, we will try to evaluate their significance in the light of our growing understanding of this specific human being's way of experiencing himself. We will not become overoptimistic because of an unexpected improvement, nor will we become exasperated by a sudden relapse into previously relinquished symptoms. We may understand how some—after one or two steps ahead—may suddenly be frightened by a renewed onslaught of self-contempt. We may lay ourselves open to the anxiety which may engulf such a newly stricken traveler on the road toward self-awareness. Being sympathetic with his despair, we have compassion for his suddenly arising powerless rage. Feeling ourselves into his situation will prevent a dangerously reassuring attitude. Yet we can communicate to him our active and encouraging "standing by" him, which is crucial, especially when he may turn against us. We may see this as an acting out of his pride which has again turned violently against his constructive forces.

UNDERSTANDING DREAMS

Deeply hidden neurotic solutions may become quite overt in the patient's dream material. What is equally pertinent, we can become aware and alerted by emotions first expressed in dreams and in relating dreams. A dream may not only help us to understand a specific solution by its content or its appearance at a particular time, or its meaning in the present situation but, most important, by its feeling qualities—its emotional intensity in an otherwise cold, detached person. If we feel an emotional resonance in ourselves to the specific feeling quality of the patient's dream it may be startling because the patient may have exhibited a lack of such feelings or have ridiculed them. Yet in dreams he may still be able to experience them in their true intensity. Often such an emotional upsurge in a dream may be the precursor of a release of conscious feeling. Again we can rely on our own deeper understanding of the sequence in which such a return to more spontaneous living may be announced. Feeling ourselves in the patient's situation we may communicate our discovery and its meanings; or something in ourselves may warn us: the patient is not yet ready to take an open stand against his unfeeling pride. If we forgo such an inner warning and interpret prematurely, he may stop dreaming or stop relating dreams.

Here, as in all other analytical communications, our intellectual awareness of change will be guided by the intuitive quality of our deeper understanding of the individual patient's capacity to take in that which may still be too upsetting to his shaky equilibrium. In singular instances, however, our own spontaneous reaction to such an emotional reawakening may be transmitted to the patient, verbally or nonverbally, explicitly or implicitly. Our understanding of his reaction to our understanding interest may set something going. This may become overt immediately, in the following hour, in a subsequent dream, or at a much later date. To register and evaluate such an experience with all our being may fortify the analytical relationship.

UNDERSTANDING THE ANALYTICAL RELATIONSHIP

If we are wholeheartedly interested, the patient may intuitively become aware of our respect for him, our sincere wish to understand him, our own stand in its various aspects. This mutuality may then give him the courage to move closer to his own constructive forces, because he now feels more secure in the common understanding of previously eclipsed or distorted aspects of himself. For the time being, he may accept himself as he is and try to understand how he became what he is. He may even become more active in examining his inner reality. But such a frank acceptance of his own imperfection may again arouse anxiety. Neurotic defenses may interfere with his wish to become emotionally alive. He may again withdraw from this stand for a constructive reorientation because anxiety may become paramount.

Understanding the individual patient's degree of alienation—the amount of his detachment and externalizing, the still-persisting adherence to narcissistic goals, the relative strength or weakness of his aliveness, the obstacles against his emerging spontaneity—will become a new task for the analyst. What we must evaluate then is the intensity of anxiety in comparison to the patient's capacity to endure its torture. Such a difficult weighing is possible only if the analyst's own feelings are wholeheartedly involved in this understanding. Here, a detached analyst will be at a loss, whereas a comprehending one, a warm human being, will stand by with all his faculties and give just as much help as a panicky patient can take. Overdoing this would lead to a renewal of dependency dynamics or to the more dangerous complete withdrawal. But with a wholehearted understanding of the analytical relationship and its intricacies, this period can become a living experience; the analyst's acceptance gives the patient the strength to move again and again toward new efforts to take a stand for himself as he is, and against those forces which obstruct his healthy development. Gradually his claims will become less and finally they can drop out. Then he will be less egocentric and more self-aware.

As his self-contempt diminishes he gains respect for himself, for the struggling human being in him. Such a freeing of oneself from the imprisonment of neurotic involvement can liberate previously eclipsed emotions. At first he may experience them only as a fleeting, abortive feeling or as physical well-being, warmth. But with the analyst's steady encouragement to live with this feeling, he may deepen such an experience. However, we will have to understand patiently his still-persisting need to condemn such feelings or his pride in embellishing them. It is self-evident that our own emotional participation will prevent a judgmental attitude. Furthermore, it will help the patient to steer free from rationalizing. Even if he is still inclined to intellectualize his present stand, we must try to understand this as the position of a man who has to find his way toward freedom after having been in prison too long. "Don't go overboard on feelings," Horney warned at this point of her lecture.

Much work must be done until the patient has overcome the experience of emptiness which usually arises in a person who gives up neurotic solutions dictated by pride, and self-contempt, and who has only incompletely reoriented himself as to his assets. The sensitive and understanding analyst will try unflaggingly to awaken the patient's numbed confidence in his own creative abilities until such a time when the troubled human being is strong enough to mobilize them for self-realization.

Karen Horney on Psychoanalytic Technique

III. EVALUATION OF CHANGE · *Ralph Slater*

Our task, as psychoanalysts, is to help our patients change. We conceive of neurosis as a character disorder, a way of life in which a person is compulsively driven in an unhealthy direction by a variety of rigid and conflicting needs. This precarious way of life begins in childhood with basic anxiety [1] and basic conflict,[2] and continues with the person's desperate and contradictory unconscious attempts to solve his inner conflict. Of these neurotic attempts at conflict solution, perhaps the most significant is the creation, in imagination, of an idealized self.[3] The idealized image becomes more real to the person than his real self, and his life becomes devoted to the attempt to actualize it. Our therapeutic aim is to help our patients change from striving mainly for self-idealizing to striving mainly for self-fulfillment.[4] Unless there is change in this direction, we cannot say that our therapeutic endeavors have been successful. It is not enough that a patient ac-

Compiled and edited by Dr. Slater from lectures on psychoanalytic technique given by Karen Horney at the American Institute for Psychoanalysis during the years 1946, 1950 and 1952. Reprinted from *The American Journal of Psychoanalysis,* XX, 1, 1960.

quires insight, that he becomes aware of something he didn't know previously—knowledge without inner change is sterile.

It is therefore essential that we evaluate the degree and nature of change in our patients if we are to assess accurately the effectiveness of our work. This is easier said than done. Many factors make it difficult to evaluate change. Among these are the following:

1. We are dependent, to a degree, on what the patient communicates to us during the analytic hours. We do not have the opportunity to observe him at home and at work, among relatives, friends, and strangers. Also, we do not interview his wife, children, teachers, employers, employees, and peers. In short, we do not have the benefit of the observations of others, including people who see a good deal of him and who may have known him for a long period of time. It should be added, however, that the fact that the analyst does not see the patient as often as a spouse, for example, also has its advantages. A certain distance and objectivity may make it possible for the analyst to recognize and evaluate changes which are not recognized by those who live with the patient and see him daily.

The patient's own statements concerning the ways in which he has or has not changed are often unreliable. For one thing, some patients are unconsciously compelled to exaggerate the degree of their improvement; they bring in reports of how much they have progressed in much the same spirit as the pupil who presents his teacher with a shiny red apple. Irrationally over-optimistic patients similarly exaggerate their progress. On the other hand, there are patients with equally powerful unconscious motives who are compelled to minimize or deny any change or improvement. Included in this group are patients who have to belittle the analyst and analysis, and those who have an intense aversion to change. In neither case can the analyst take at face value his patient's statements about progress and change. A second consideration is that the patient's and the analyst's concepts of progress often do not coincide. Thus, a patient will feel gratified because he has become increasingly successful in taking revenge upon his detractors, that is, on those who hurt his pride or frustrate his claims. In such a case, the analyst will recognize that his patient has changed, but not in the direction of self-fulfillment. This will also apply in those situations where the patient's change is on the basis of compulsive compliance, and where the change is a behavioral but not an inner one.

2. The analyst's neurotic tendencies, to the degree that they persist, will warp his judgment and make it difficult or even impossible for him to estimate the extent and nature of the patient's change. Thus, the analyst with some persistence of resignation as a way of life, which includes an aversion to and a disbelief in change, may be blind to evidences of it in the patient. On the other hand, a therapist's need to cure all his patients, and to do so as rapidly as possible, may make him see more change than has in fact occurred. In these instances, I am referring to neurotic residuals in the doctor. In addition to these, it is inherently difficult to recognize changes in the patient, since they are often subtle and slow to develop.

3. External changes may affect the patient, making it difficult for the analyst to determine whether the person's improvement (or, for that matter, his worsening) is due to them, or to the analytic process, or to both in varying degrees. Such factors as marriage, divorce, the death of a relative or friend, and economic and occupational suc-

cess or failure may bring about changes in a patient. There are certain patients who are more likely than is warranted to attribute change in themselves to external factors. Analysts are less likely to do so, since they are not compelled to externalize to the same degree.

We may attempt to determine change in the patient by considering evidence from two points of view. The first of these is: is there less of the neurotic in the patient? We would raise and attempt to answer questions such as the following. In general, is the person less driven by compulsion? Is he, for example, less pushed around by needs indiscriminately to please and placate others, to subordinate himself to others, to provoke abuse? Is he less compelled to belittle and disparage people, to prove himself superior to and triumph vindictively over them? Is he less coerced into attaining perfect freedom and self-sufficiency? Is he less anxious and less driven by an insatiable ambition? Does he make fewer irrational claims on people and on life? Is there a diminution in the rigidity and extent of his perfectionistic standards, and the severity of his self-contempt and self-accusation? Does he externalize less— that is, is there a lessening of the need to attribute his inner feelings and thoughts to people and institutions other than himself? Is there less need to pretend to virtues that he really does not possess? To the degree that the answer to these and similar questions is "yes," to that extent the analyst can feel than the patient has changed, and in the direction of increasing psychic health.

As examples of this "less of the neurotic," I will mention two patients. The first of these had experienced giving Christmas presents to her fellow employees as a torture, because her presents had to be "absolutely the best. I couldn't even consider the possibility of mine being other

246 · Advances in Psychoanalysis

than the best." Some years later she was able to give a Christmas gift which was nice, although not the absolute best, and "it didn't kill me. Quite a relief." At the same time this patient noted a decrease in her sensitivity to criticism. "Things don't bother me so much anymore—I'm less sensitive—I'm not hurt so deeply and so long by remarks." The other patient illustrates a decrease in unconscious pretending and self-deceiving. She said, "I'm not so sweet and self-sacrificing as I appear; underneath, I want quite a lot, but I want only expensive things, though I pretend otherwise."

The other point of view is a positive one, namely, is there more evidence of healthy thinking, feeling, and acting in the patient? In order to arrive at an answer, we would again raise and attempt to answer questions such as these: Does the patient sleep better, eat better, feel happier? Does he have more satisfying and enjoyable relationships with his fellows? Is he more spontaneous, more alive? Does he feel more deeply, and are his feelings appropriate and sustained? Is he able to express tender as well as angry feelings? Is he more honest with himself and others, more dependable, more courageous? Does he recognize and accept assets and limitations in himself and others? Is he able to work more creatively, in a more sustained and satisfying manner, and on his own initiative? Can he constructively criticize himself and others, and is he able to take criticism of himself and his work without undue upset? Can he enjoy both work and leisure? Can he take a stand, or yield, in accordance with his own inclinations and the requirements of his situation? Does he begin to question his standards, to ask himself, for example, is it really valuable, always, to be hard and tough and ready to do battle? To the degree that the answers to such questions are affirmative, to that degree we can feel convinced that the patient has changed in the direction of healthier living.

Evidence of increasing health may be found in the patient's dreaming. There may be a change in the pattern—thus, a person who rarely if ever dreams may begin to dream more, or rather, to remember more dreams, bring them in, and work on them. Conversely, a patient who has flooded the analyst with a super-abundance of material may begin to bring in fewer dreams. (Exactly the same can be said about memories of childhood experiences.) There may be a change in the attitude toward dreams, in the direction of increasing interest in and more productive associations to them. Also, change in the dream content may indicate change in the direction of increasing health. For example, dreams in which the person is a spectator of conflict may be replaced by dreams in which he is an active participant. Or, something new, or growing and developing, may appear for the first time. Something living may appear where before there was deadness. Consider the dream of a woman who for a long time had complied with all demands, including unfair ones, while inwardly resenting the people whom she obeyed. She finally became able to say no to claims made on her, with a resultant decrease in resentment. In a dream she saw herself in a coffin. Suddenly her dead self in the coffin came to life and sat up, to everyone's surprise.

In the evolving doctor-patient relationship, the doctor will find evidence of change in the patient. Here the analyst's conclusions will be based on his own observations, feelings, and thoughts, as well as the patient's actions and words, and therefore will be more valid than if they were based solely on the latter. In the beginning, the patient experiences the analyst as magic helper, adversary, and intruder. He may be unduly conciliatory, hostile, defensive, and secretive. If the analysis proceeds successfully, the patient's attitudes change and this change is one that the analyst can see, hear, and sense. An over-effusive gratitude may gradually be replaced by an appropriate appreciation for help given. Defensiveness diminishes and the person becomes more honest and open. Fears of ridicule and contempt decrease, and the patient becomes more willing and able to expose what he has had to cover up to the analyst and to himself. Hostile tendencies to disparage and frustrate the analyst-adversary are gradually replaced by a sense of cooperation with another, helping human being in the effort of self-discovery. A hitherto frightened and timid person may become able to disagree with and even to criticize the therapist. Or, a cold and withdrawn person may become able to feel and express positive feelings toward the analyst. As the patient's need for rigid self-control diminishes, his previously not-so-free associations become freer, and there is less compulsive intellectualizing and more letting go during the analytic hours.

I could go on listing many changes in a patient's words about and attitudes toward the analyst, which the latter can observe and feel. From what has already been mentioned, however, it should be obvious that the analytic relationship offers the analyst an excellent opportunity to observe and evaluate change in his patient. I would add to this that visible changes in the patient's appearance are also available to the analyst. I recall a patient, a young woman who always struck me as being poorly dressed; her clothes never seemed to hang right. During the analytic work she came to realize that she thought of herself as closely resembling a certain movie actress in appearance and physique. Actually, the actress was three or four inches taller than my patient. After the patient accepted the fact that she was really 5'2" tall, not 5'6", she bought clothes which fit properly, and there was a distinct change in her appearance, which became aesthetically more pleasing. Similarly, there may be a change in a person's posture—for example, from bent-over and cringing to erect and confident. A person's eyes may change from dead and fishy to alive and warm. A voice may gain in assurance, while at the same time, there may be a noticeable decrease in restlessness and fidgeting. Here again, I could go on listing such changes, but it is already clear that the analyst can be guided in his task of evaluating change by observation of his patient's appearance and behavior.

To summarize and conclude, the analyst who wants to assess the effectiveness of his therapy must attempt to evaluate change in his patient. He must do this with some regularity—for example, every three or every six months—otherwise, he may not do it at all. He will look for evidence that his patient is more spontaneous and less compulsive in his acting, feeling, and thinking. In doing this, he will pay attention not only to what the patient does and doesn't say, but to the totality of the patient's response—to what the person says and how he says it, what he does in work, how he gets along with people, what he dreams, how he dresses, and so on. And, of course, the analyst will also pay attention to his own feelings. An attempt must be made to determine whether or not a patient's progress is proportionate to the time and effort invested. In making this determination, the individual analyst's experience is invaluable. If there has been no progress, or less than might reasonably have been expected, the analyst must ask himself such questions as, what in the patient stands in the way of more growing, and what other ways and means can I use in tackling the difficulty. Such questioning and evaluating is valuable because it is in the service of determining the effectiveness of therapy, and of promoting ways to increase its effectiveness.

REFERENCES

1. Horney, K., *The Neurotic Personality of Our Time,* W. W. Norton, New York, 1937.
2. Horney, K., *Our Inner Conflicts,* W. W. Norton, New York, 1945.
3. *Ibid.,* Chapter VI.
4. Slater, R., "Aims of Psychoanalytic Therapy," *The American Journal of Psychoanalysis,* XVI.

INDEX

human relationships, functional and personal compared, 65
Hunt, W. A., 149
hypochondriasis, 160
hysteria, 147

Ibsen, Henrik, 235
id, 185–86
idealized image, 94, 184, 189, 191–92, 202–03, 205, 210–11; creation of as attempt at neurotic solution of conflict, 242
impotence as symptom of anxiety, 146–47
individuation, 150
"Initial Interview, The" (Cantor), 223
inner experiences, paucity of, 36–38, 47–64; manifestations of, 48ff.; influence on life and therapy, 48ff.; patient's awareness of and attitudes toward, 48ff., 52; and suffering, 53; and psychoanalytic therapy, 54ff.; and the neurotic process, 56
integrating, process of, 111–12
integration, 149–51; and growth, 67; concept of, 111; tension producing patterns of, 117
intellectualizing, as blockage to therapeutic process, 54–56
International Journal of Psychoanalysis, 8–9
"Interpretations" (Cantor), 223

Jevons, W. S., 90
Jones, Ernest, 7–8

Kahn, E., 134
Karenina, Anna, 208–09
Kierkegaard, Soren, 51, 63
Kinsey, A., 161, 169
Körperbau und Charakter (Kretschmer), 9
Kretschmer, Ernst, 9
Kubie, L., 135

Landis, C., 149
language, evolution of and the development of the body concept, 155
love and sex, 164ff.
love as curative force, 171

MacMurray, J., 65
Magic Mountain, The (Mann), 156
Man Against Himself (Menninger), 151, 201
manic depressive, 213
Mann, Thomas, 156
masochism, 126
masturbation, as symptom of anxiety, 146–47, 160
Maugham, Somerset, 173
Menninger, Karl, 151, 201
mental illness as technique of self-preservation, 109ff.
Mill, John Stuart, 90
Mittelmann and Wolf, 134, 140–41
Moro, E., 149
Munroe, Ruth, 13

narcissism, as love of the idealized image, 212
negative body image, 171–72
neurasthenia, 160
Neurosis and Human Growth (Horney), 16–17
neurotic and analyst, relations between, 32
neurotic drive and sex, 165ff.
neurotic feelings of abuse, 29ff.; unawareness of, 32ff.; variations in attitudes toward, 33ff.; as defense function, 39; sources of, 43
neurotic guilt, 170ff.
neurotic love, 208
neurotic need for self-sufficiency, 126
Neurotic Personality of Our Time, The (Horney), 11–12
neurotic pride, 31, 160, 202, 207, 216–17; in invulnerability, 33; in